HAPPI KITCHE MAINE

RECIPES FROM REAL WOMEN

Paula Boyer Rougny

HAPPINESS IS A KITCHEN IN MAINE

RECIPES FROM REAL WOMEN

HAPPINESS IS A KITCHEN IN MAINE

RECIPES FROM REAL WOMEN

Paula Boyer Rougny

Illustrations by Betsy Fear

Peapatch Press
147 River Road
Woolwich, Maine 04579

Copyright 1998
Peapatch Press
147 River Road, Woolwich, Maine 04579
peapatch@gwi.net

Illustrations by Betsy Fear
Design & Layout by Ludwig Graphics, Bangor, Maine

Library of Congress Catalog Card No.: 97-095134

Happiness Is A Kitchen In Maine.

ISBN 0-9660852-0-5

Printed and bound in the USA

10 9 8 7 6 5 4 3 2 1

Copyright Acknowledgments

"Recuerdo" by Edna St.Vincent Millay. From COLLECTED POEMS, HarperCollins.
Copyright 1922, 1950 by Edna St.Vincent Millay.

"The Owl and The Pussy-Cat" and "There Was An Old Person of Blythe"
by Edward Lear, 1862. From the COMPLETE NONSENSE BOOK,
copyright 1912 by Constance, Lady Strachey

Acknowledgments

I thank everyone who taught by example of creative thinking: my mother Regina Hongisto Hufford Jones, a distinguished cook who inspired me to travel, literally and in books; my French mother-in-law, Juliette Rougny, whose cooking was exquisite, herb infused, and gathered from her garden; Françoise Rougny Woodard and Jacqueline Brisset Mykytiuk, superb cooks of both their native French and other cuisines.

Thank you to the only grandparents I knew, Thomas and May Harper Boyer; he gardened, she put up vegetables like works of art and lined them on shelves in a cool, dark pantry.

My gratitude to Joujou Rougny, who continues to enlighten me about vegetarian and dairy-free cooking; to Maggie Kolvenbach, who showed me how to make rosettes with sugar frosting; to the late Helen MacInnes, 18 year resident of China and weaver extraordinaire, who spent a Thursday afternoon showing us how to shop and cook Chinese.

To the long ago Girl Scout leader who taught a group of little girls how to cook vegetables. I was so captivated by the one-inch-of-water method that it is the only Scout meeting I can remember. To the 7th grade home ec teacher who revealed the mysteries of making carrot salad.

All my heart to Cézanne's runty apples, which I thrilled to on canvas but considered abstract (apples are big and red). At age 20 I went to France to study and learned that apples are small and runty and taste delicious.

Thanks to chef Norm Brillant, who inspired me on the job and came to my house when I was trying to invent a scone from one whose recipe was off limits. He alternately tasted my scone and the one from the bakery and said "Use pastry flour."

For non-culinary help I thank Julie Zimmerman of Biddle Press, Kerry Leichtman of Dancing Bear Books, Irene Howe, Amy Ludwig of Ludwig Graphics, and everyone at Maine Writers and Publishers Alliance.

Thank you Betsy Fear for the fine illustrations and thank you Elizabeth Walsh Rougny for the straight-on editorial advice. My gratitude to Dr. Chris Northrup at Women to Women for telling a class, "Sit down and enjoy a relationship with your food."

I thank all the public libraries I have haunted for recipes and lore, and the handful of restaurant kitchens that let me watch the high tension work. This includes the galley kitchen of a speeding train.

Hugs to the Thursday bunch who give me culinary advice, discuss the fate of the world, respond to my questions (sometimes all at once), dine in and out with me, talk woman talk, exchange recipes, loan books and make me laugh: Bobby Johnston, Rosemary Campbell, Tim Vrooman, Jini Milam, Joan Lipfert, Lois Hilliker, Gretchen Shaw, and twins Sue Blair and Helen Boynton.

Most of these recipes serve six persons.

Contents

Why People Move To Maine

In practical matters, especially in the kitchen,
where one really should have an open fire,
there are to be found mysterious ecstasies
of which the purely functionally-minded
never dream. Simple things hold the secret,
not complicated ones.

C. G. Jung, 1934

The great Swiss psychologist knew why people move to
Maine: pine forests, wild blueberries, farmers' markets that
bloom in the spring, eagles that float in the sky. Simple things.

Most Mainers direct their lives in harmony with the seasons. Both natives and in-migrants* know the pleasure of icy
spring soil brushed against fingertips. They enjoy the luxury
of a pantry on a cool north wall, summertime harvest from their
own backyards, and boots that leave clumps of clay inside the
kitchen door, or beyond it in the shed.

Most older kitchens lead into an attached shed that shel-
ters an inside outhouse and such appurtenances as firewood,
sleds, clothesline, canoe, and tools. Some sheds lead into more
sheds and, the dénouement, an enchanted cathedral called
barn. The arrangement is known as connected architecture.
It's one of the simple things that holds the secret.

I would be honored to spend a year in any number of
Maine kitchens, observing the occupants and filming a docu-
mentary to be called Mysterious Ecstasies of the Maine Kitchen.
It would include the following scenes:

~ *Anna Shoos Away a Moose with her apron*
~ *The Kittens in the Warming Oven at Bill and Alice's*
~ *The Fog Rolls In and Out and In as Nancy Stirs Jam*

Not all recipes in this book originated in Maine. Too many in-migrants spent earlier lives working in cities all over the map. Too many natives — Bill and Alice, for example — earned a living elsewhere before returning as young retirees. Even in the 19th century, when the Wabanakis gathered fiddleheads, and the French came down from Quebec, and the wives of sea captains circumnavigated the globe, Maine cooking was full of surprises.

The kitchens themselves are full of surprises: farmhouse kitchens with old slate sinks; summer cottages where green oilcloth is tacked onto countertops and gingham curtains stand in for cupboard doors; kitchens with ancient beehive ovens; sunny, open kitchens in solar-powered nests; vernacular kitchens in the north woods, where Canada lines three sides and townships have numbers instead of names.

For some Mainers the stove of choice is a woodburner. Though most of the state's one million year-round residents (two million more arrive in summer) rely on tech, the woodburning contingent warrants mention because theirs is a useful skill. Woodburning cooks manipulate the heat of a single surface into stir-fry high and stockpot simmer, simultaneously. They honor the requisites of stack, split, and carry (firewood in, ashes out). By choice. Because useful skills are one of the simple things.

* *People who move by choice, because Maine is a state of mind.*

Vegetables Plain and Basic

ARTICHOKES

Trim tough outer leaves. (There may be three, four, five.) Cut off end of stem so that artichoke stands upright. Cover with water, bring to a boil, simmer. Drain. Stand each artichoke in the center of a salad plate like a graceful monument. Tear off petals with hands, dip each in an oil and vinegar dressing, or in a lemon-adulterated mayonnaise, and teeth-scrape the petal-paste from each. When the last of it has vanished and you have a heap of spent petals on your plate, cut the fuzzies away from the choke and devour the round, succulent heart with a fork.

ASPARAGUS

Do not refrigerate asparagus for more than a day or two. It should be cooked spanking fresh.

Snap off tough lower half of each spear; your sense of touch tells you where. Steam in a steamer basket 5 to 8 minutes. Or drop into a pot of boiling water, boil gently, uncovered, until thickest part is just tender, 4 to 6 minutes — less if you harvested it from your garden that day.

GREEN (ALIAS STRING) BEANS

Buy slender, not overweight, beans. Snap off ends unless beans are deliriously small and garden fresh. Make lengthwise slits in any that are on the stout side.

Steam 4 to 6 minutes. Or drop into a pot of boiling water, boil gently, uncovered, 2 to 5 minutes depending on thickness. KEEPING THE POT UNCOVERED KEEPS THE COLOR IN THE VEGGIE, ANY VEGGIE.

BEANS, DRIED (See Grains and Beans as Main Dish)

BEANS, FRESH SHELL (broad, lima, kidney)

Remove beans from pods, place in a pot with water to cover, bring to a boil, simmer, covered, 10 to 20 minutes depending on size of beans.

BEETS

Cut off greens to within one or two inches of the beet. Do not cut off roots. (Cut a beet to the quick and the red will drain away, nutrients in tow, during the cooking.) Cover with water, bring to a boil, simmer covered, 25 to 50 minutes depending on the size of the beets. Test with knife.

BROCCOLI

Cut off and discard tough bottom part of stalks. Pull off leaves. Cut broccoli heads into florets. Steam 3 to 10 minutes depending on whether you have cut teensy or chunky florets. Or drop into a large pot of boiling water, boil gently, uncovered, two to five minutes, depending on how small you have made the pieces.

BRUSSELS SPROUTS

Remove any discolored leaves, trim base. Steam 8 to 12 minutes. Or drop into a large pot of boiling water, boil gently, uncovered, four to eight minutes, depending on size.

CABBAGE

Cut cabbage in quarters, cut away core. Slice into wedges, drop into a large pot of boiling water, boil gently, uncovered, 6 to 10 minutes, depending on whether your wedges are thin or chunky. Steam a few minutes longer, or cut cabbage into fine slices and sauté in olive oil or butter for 5 minutes. Caraway seeds add crunchy companionship.

CHINESE CABBAGE has a lighter, more exquisite taste and requires less cooking time, about 3 minutes sautéed.

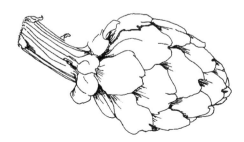

CARROTS

Trim and roughly peel carrots. Slice straight across, on the diagonal (makes comely ovals), or into thin slices or dice. Cut smaller carrots lengthwise or leave whole.

Steam 5 to 10 minutes. Or drop into a pot of boiling water, boil gently, uncovered, 2 to 8 minutes, depending on size of pieces.

Raw shredded carrot is a happiness color when added to green salad or cole slaw.

CAULIFLOWER

Remove leaves, cut into florets. Steam 4 to 8 minutes. Or drop into a large pot of boiling water, boil gently, uncovered, 3 to 6 minutes.

CORN (on and off the cob)

Drop ears of corn, minus their rich silky wraps, into a large pot of boiling water, boil gently, uncovered, 4 to 7 minutes. Field-fresh corn cooks in a wink, corn trucked cross-country longer.

Cool leftover ears to room temperature, secure in a covered container, refrigerate. To reheat, sauté in a speck of olive oil or an olive oil-butter mix with or without a little chopped green or red pepper and onion.

EGGPLANT

is a vegetable people use more in casseroles with onions, tomatoes and peppers than on its own. But it is so exceptionally fresh, small and tender during the local harvest season that it is an act of dishonor not to prepare it solo.

Trim green tops, peel (or don't) and slice into rounds or half rounds. Read *The Eggplant Has a Secret*, next page. Sauté slices in a touch of olive oil for 5 or 6 minutes, turning once. Drain on paper towels. Drizzle more oil into the skillet as needed.

If you feel theatrical, cut eggplant *lengthwise* into thin, even slices (do not peel). Sauté two or three at a time — more will not fit into one sauté pan — until crisp. Scatter with a fresh herb of choice.

THE EGGPLANT HAS A SECRET

The glossiness of the eggplant is so other-worldly that at harvest time the purpley things deserve to be heaped into great wooden bowls with that other glistening late-summer miracle, the green pepper. The visual appeal begs to be painted onto canvas.

The secret? *Bitter juices.* Ninety-seven percent of eggplants have them, the exception being small, young, garden fresh ones. What it means is that after you peel and slice the vegetable you should dump the pieces into a colander, salt them on both sides, and leave them to brood for a half hour. Don't look for a waterfall of juices; they tend to materialize as beads, although there is some dripping. Blot the slices dry with a kitchen towel and proceed with the operation.

FIDDLEHEADS

The fiddlehead fern grows wild in Maine in damp shady terrain. It tastes like asparagus-not-really and is harvested during a brief spring season. If you spy fiddleheads as green as can be in a store or at a farmer's market, rinse in cold water as you pull off the brown "paper" that may cling to them. Drop into a pot of boiling water and boil, uncovered, 5 minutes. Or steam 7 minutes.

GARLIC

has lavished health on all comers for 6,000 years. Mince, press, or chop raw garlic into salad dressings and other sauces. Sauté but *do not burn*, add to soups and stir-fries. Bake to eat on its own. Smear onto slices of country bread.

To bake, place individual cloves of unpeeled garlic into a baking dish, drizzle with olive oil and, if you like, sprinkle with salt and pepper and a herb of choice. Bake in a preheated 300° oven 30 minutes. To devour, press each clove out of its skin.

LEEKS

are one of the grimiest customers the cook may hope to encounter. Cut off all but one or two inches of green tops, peel tough outer skin. Trim root end and, to dislodge inner dirt (it lurks out of sight), make a lengthwise slit halfway down the leek from the green end. Rinse under cold running water.

Place leeks, which have drained dry, in a heavy skillet or wide pot with a lid. Add water but not enough to completely cover the vegetables. Bring to a boil, simmer, covered, 12 to 15 minutes. Gently transfer onto plates. If you steam: add a few minutes to the cooking time.

MUSHROOMS

Wipe with a damp towel to remove dirt, slice off bottom sliver of stem. Slice, sauté in butter or olive oil 3 minutes. Excellent sautéed with chopped scallions or onions, seasoned with salt and pepper and served as a filling for an omelet or spooned over couscous or rice or added to soup. Raw mushrooms comprise good salad fixings.

Experiment with different varieties, both fresh and dried, even mushrooms that come in jars of marinade. They are interesting characters.

ONIONS

Primarily used as flavor enhancers for other foods, onions are also worthy of being the treat du jour. Peel papery outer skins of yellow onions, cover with water, bring to a boil and simmer, covered, about 20 minutes. Serve with butter, salt, pepper, and waves of green minced parsley.

Or put peeled whole onions in a baking dish with butter or olive oil smeared all over them and in the dish. Sprinkle with salt and pepper. Bake, covered, in a preheated 400° oven 45 to 60 minutes.

PARSNIPS

Scrape, cut into sticks or chunks, steam 8 to 12 minutes, or drop into a large pot of boiling water and boil gently, uncovered, 5 to 10 minutes, depending on whether you have cut matchsticks or firewood.

PEAS

Shell peas, steam 3 minutes. Or drop into a pot of boiling water and boil gently, uncovered, 1 minute. SNOW PEAS (with pod): Simmer or stir-fry 3 to 4 minutes.

POTATOES

To bake (Idaho or Russet), scrub off dirt, puncture once on each side with a fork, bake in a preheated 425° oven 45 to 60 minutes. Test by piercing with a paring knife. Cover with water, bring to a boil, simmer covered. Small whole potatoes will cook in 15 to 20 minutes, medium ones 30 to 40. Peel or not. Shorten the cooking time by cutting larger potatoes in half, or slicing or dicing. Thin-sliced potatoes cook in 3 to 4 minutes.

FRENCH FRIES are so available as take-out that you lack the capitalistic spirit if you prepare them from scratch. But when you feel radical: Peel firm potatoes. Cut into sticks by whatever method is available. (I have a 1920s "Vite-Frite" from France that transcends a potato into delicate *frites* (pronounced freet) with the efficiency of a guillotine.) Place sticks in a bowl of cold water for 30 minutes. Drain. Dry thoroughly. Heat several inches of corn oil in a heavy pot until hot but not smoking. Test oil by dropping in a piece of potato or bread. If the offering sizzles, the oil is ready.

Add potatoes — no crowding — in a frying basket or loose in the pot if you have a wire ladle. Cook *frites* several minutes, until golden. Do not stir. Remove, drain on paper towels; sprinkle with salt. Keep each batch in a warm oven until all are cooked. Save leftover oil, covered, in the frying pot or another container, in a cool spot, for future cooking of anything you may wish to deep fry. Trash after it becomes unsavory with blackened veggie scraps.

LEFTOVER POTATOES: Mince potatoes and sauté with a little minced

7

onion, salt, pepper in hot oil or a butter-oil mix. As you cook, use a spatula to pat the top and sides to shape a fat little cake. When your cake is crisp on the bottom, flip and fry on the other side. If it is large you may have to divide or quarter it, flip each piece and reconstruct. Serve with catsup and say HASHBROWN.

RUTABAGAS (See Turnips)

SPINACH

Place in a pot with just the rinse water that clings to the leaves. Simmer 2 to 3 minutes (give it a stir after one minute). Or steam 4 to 6 minutes. Spinach has a crush on fresh lemon juice; use lots of it, with butter or olive oil.

SQUASH

Squash greets us in two categories: summer (zucchini, yellow, pattypan) and winter (acorn, butternut, Hubbard, pumpkin, spaghetti).

Once picked off the vine, SUMMER SQUASH does not appreciate being 1) stored and 2) overcooked. Cut summer squash into thin slices or on the diagonal, sauté in a touch of olive oil or an oil-butter mix for 3 to 4 minutes. Chopped garlic may be added after a few minutes - be careful not to burn it crisp. The grand finale is salt and pepper.

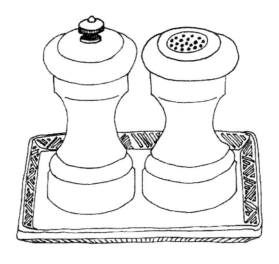

WINTER SQUASH: Cut acorn squash in half crosswise for a scallop edge design. Smear rim and interior with butter and sprinkle with salt and pepper. Bake rightside up or upside down in a preheated 350° oven 45 to 60 minutes. (If you bake it upright, take a sliver off the bottom so the squash doesn't teeter in baking pan or dinner plate.

Cut a butternut squash into 4 or 5 chunks, scoop out seeds and fibers. Now cut into uniform, or as uniform as a butternut will give you permission for, smaller chunks, place in a pot with water barely to cover. Bring to a boil, cover, simmer 4 or 5 minutes or till pulp is tender when pierced with a fork. Drain. When cool enough to handle, pare away the softened rinds. Mash pulp with butter, salt and pepper. Fresh lime juice adds youth and romance.

PUMPKIN PIE represents the most seductive use of squash in the galaxy. Buy a small, sweet, 4 pound sugar pumpkin. You do not want a large jack-o-lantern variety or a small "decorator" one. A 4 pound sugar pumpkin will yield 3 or 4 cups of cooked pulp, which is too much for one pie and may or may not stretch to make two. Serve the excess as a vegetable with butter, salt and pepper, or indulge in a mini pie.

To cook: Cut a slice off both top and bottom of pumpkin. Hold steady, pare shell from top to bottom, turning pumpkin as you proceed. Cut in half or in quarters, scoop out seeds and fiber with a spoon (a cheap one with a thin edge works beautifully). Cut pumpkin into more or less uniform chunks, simmer in water barely to cover 10 to 15 minutes depending on size of pieces. Drain, pare, mash.

PUMPKIN SEED SNACKS: After scraping seeds out of shell (any kind of pumpkin), rinse under running water in a colander, picking out and discarding the stringy stuff. Pat dry. Scatter into a shallow baking pan and stir in 1 T corn oil and 1 t salt for each cup of seeds. Bake in a preheated 250° oven one hour. Stir twice during baking. When cool, turn into a jar with a tight cover.

SWEET POTATOES

THIS VEGGIE IS LOADED WITH NUTRIENTS: VITAMIN C, CALCIUM, IRON, THIAMIN.

Bake whole sweet potatoes in a preheated 350° oven 45 to 60 minutes, depending on size. Test for doneness with a paring knife, pushing it through to the center. Transfer to dinner plates and let each person slit open his own.

TOMATOES

Botanically a fruit, the tomato is America's most widely grown "vegetable." But don't buy them out of season, when the taste is paste. For winter consumption, buy canned or dried tomatoes, or freeze or can your own during your area's harvest season.

SLICED: Arrange slightly overlapping, on a platter. Season with salt and pepper, sprinkle with fresh cilantro, drizzle with dressing.

BAKED: Slice off top one-third of tomato and present it to the compost pile. Place tomatoes, sides touching, in a shallow baking dish. Chop garlic and push several pieces into each tomato. Top with a drizzle of olive oil, salt and pepper and — optional — grated Parmesan cheese. Bake in a preheated 350° oven 45 minutes to one hour. Sprinkle with a chopped fresh herb. At the end of the season you can bake green tomatoes. Leave in the oven 15 or 20 minutes longer than you would red ones.

PROVENÇALE: Sauté two chopped cloves garlic in 2 T olive oil. Add five or six ripe, peeled, broken-up tomatoes. Lower heat and cook gently 10 minutes. Off heat, toss in a handful of croutons and freshly minced parsley.

ALL TIME WINNER: Make a BLT with mayo on toasted rye. Dill pickle on the side.

TURNIPS AND RUTABAGAS

Turnips are small rutabagas and rutabagas large turnips. Turnips look good intact with pot roasts, stews, and corned beef cabbage.

Scrub small turnips (peel larger ones, and peel rutabagas), cut into chunks or just in half if they are particularly small and young. Cut rutabagas into uniform chunks. Drop into a large pot of boiling water and boil gently, uncovered, 8 to 10 minutes or until tender. Pierce with the tip of a paring knife to test. Or steam, which takes a bit longer. Serve with butter, salt and pepper. Lime juice mixed into mashed turnips or rutabagas also comes to the aid of these not wildly popular veggies. CREAM, IT GOES WITHOUT SAYING, MAKES EVERYTHING TASTE BETTER, and the world is happy when turnips are whipped up with butter, cream, salt and pepper.

STIR-FRY

Used as both a noun and a verb, "stir-fry" describes a method of cooking that produces bright color and crisp taste. It can refer to anything from a single veggie to an entire dinner in a skillet.

To open the show you start with a skillet (or wok) and a tablespoon or so of olive or another oil, or an oil-butter mix. Forget recipes. Have edibles at the ready.

Cut — *shape* — vegetables in goodly chunks. In contrast to a sauté, which asks for fine chopping and high heat for quick, incomplete cooking (you go on to add the sautéed items to other ingredients and further cooking), a stir-fry wants coarser chopping, attention to looks, and heat that may rise and fall as you proceed, with the cooking vessel occasionally — briefly — covered to insure that all contents cook through.

The shapes you carve are arbitrary: carrot ovals, tofu cubes (see page 14 for pressing out moisture), long slender green beans, whole shrimp, onions and olives in rings, capped or whole mushrooms. A variety of shapes creates visual pleasure, as does the color. When you shop, envision RED pepper, BLACK beans, WHITE cauliflower, ORANGE carrots, PINK shrimp, GREEN-EDGED WHITE zucchini, and, tying it all together, the muted tones of rice and mushrooms.

You can use all or a selection of the previous page. After you've doused the heat or are about to do so, you can stir in cashews, seeds, sherry, or a freshly chopped herb. Serve tamari or another sauce on the side.

OPTION   is a wise tool to use in becoming a stir-fry cook (omelet maker or cake decorator). To watch someone rustle up a gorgeous meal in one skillet is a more valuable lesson than reading 10 books on the subject. Instructions that may raise questions on the printed page become clear with observation. That's why cooking lessons are so much fun.

DENSER   vegetables (carrots) take longer to cook than less dense ones (asparagus) and chunks take longer than thin slices. Leftover rice, beans or pasta need only a warming. Use your head *and* a degree of abandon: add the denser stuff earlier so it cooks longer. Stir in leftovers or smoked fish at the last minute.

SKEWER-GRILL

Oil skewers (any oil; the idea is to grease the pole), thread with whole scallops or shrimp, fat strips of green or red peppers, onion chunks, whole cherry tomatoes, mushrooms, and fat slices of summer squash. When skewers are threaded, which you do with an eye for color manipulation, brush with an oil and vinegar dressing. Set straightaway to sizzling on a hot grill, turning once or twice for even cooking. To eat, each diner pushes the goodies off the skewer onto his plate.

The above is the merest introduction to skewers. The curious cook may want to educate herself in such advanced studies as marinating, blanching (precooking of larger veggies such as whole potatoes) and other artful designs.

Vegetables
All Dressed
Up To Go

CABBAGE ROLLS POT LUCK SUPPER

Excellent for pot luck suppers because it contains no meat. (Maine pot lucks are rife with vegetarians and their little vegetarian children.)

8 large cabbage leaves*	2 T herbs or spices of choice
16 oz package tofu	1 egg, beaten
1 T mustard	16 oz good tomato sauce
10 oz package chopped spinach	Parmesan cheese
1 onion, minced	Paper thin lemon slices
1/2 cup uncooked natural rice	Fresh parsley or dill

PREP WORK: Gently dislodge cabbage leaves and place in a very large bowl. Add boiling water to cover. Set aside, occasionally pushing under unsubmerged leaf sections.

Sandwich about half the tofu (8 oz) between two plates, setting a heavy object on the top plate in order to press the tofu, which cooks up better after its spongy disposition has dried out. Refrigerate remaining tofu in water for use on another day. Leave your press in position for 15 or 20 minutes, drain. Crumble tofu, stir in mustard, press moisture from thawed spinach.

COOKING: Sauté onion in 1 T olive or another oil in a large pot. Add rice, 1 cup water, herb(s) or spice(s) of choice, salt and pepper to taste. Bring to a boil, cover, simmer until rice is tender and water absorbed, about 20 minutes. Off heat, stir in spinach and tofu-mustard mix. Cool slightly, stir in egg.

Drain cabbage leaves and carefully cut away tough stem sections. Place approximately 1/3 cup filling in the center of each leaf, roll up. Cabbage leaves rebel at uniformity and no two leaves will roll up to look alike. Place seam-side down in a greased baking dish — a round one if possible, to please the variety of rounded shapes nestled within it.

Pour tomato sauce over rolls. Sprinkle with Parmesan to taste. Arrange a few slices of lemon over the surface for cosmetics. Bake, covered with lid or foil, in a preheated 350° oven 30 minutes. Remove cover, bake 30 minutes longer. Sprinkle with minced parsley or dill for a beautiful presentation.

---

* It usually takes two heads of cabbage to render eight good-sized leaves.

CABBAGE CASSEROLE WITH ATTITUDE

The vinegar is the ingredient that lifts this dish into the stars. Don't overdo it: two tablespoons, not a drop more.

4 or 5 potatoes	1 ½ cups cottage cheese
2 onions, chopped	1 cup plain yogurt
4 cups cabbage, shredded	Salt and pepper to taste
2 T butter + 2 T olive oil	2 T vinegar
2 T fresh dill, chopped	Fresh parsley to taste
2 T caraway seeds	Paprika to taste

Peel and cook potatoes. Sauté onions and cabbage in butter-oil mix in a large pot for 10 minutes. Stir in dill and caraway seeds, cook another minute. Cover, turn off heat, let rest 15 minutes.

Mash together potatoes, cottage cheese, yogurt, salt and pepper. Stir into cabbage pot. Stir in vinegar. Turn into a buttered casserole, bake uncovered in a preheated 350° oven 45 minutes or until the casserole bubbles and sizzles. Sprinkle with chopped parsley and paprika for an eclectic green and red design.

CARROTS FOUR SONS

One of my favorite cartoons shows a woman working in a kitchen that has all the usual appliances plus a computer terminal. She is saying, "I do a little cooking, a little baking, and I manage portfolios with assets of $50 million a year." Barbara, who lives in Corinth, personifies the woman in the cartoon. For many years she prepared this dish frequently because it WAS THE ONLY WAY HER FOUR BOYS WOULD EAT COOKED CARROTS.

The recipe turns into a large casserole indeed, so if you don't have four growing kids divide it in half and it will feed four adults.

2 lbs carrots (15 to 20 if medium-size)
1 stick butter
1/2 lb grated Velveeta
1 tube Ritz crackers (about 35)

Scrape and slice carrots, bring to boil in a pot of salted water, boil at full roll, uncovered, 5 to 10 minutes or until just tender (boys don't eat mushy carrots). In the meantime melt butter over low heat. Add Velveeta, stirring.

Drain carrots, rinse with cold water to stop the cooking, return to the pot, pour in the butter/cheese mix and stir vigorously to coat every carrot. Turn into a buttered casserole, top with crushed crackers.

Bake in a preheated 350° oven 20 to 30 minutes or until crisp. If you do the prep work early in the day and refrigerate the casserole, be sure to bring it to room temperature before sliding into the oven.

CÉLERI RÉMOULADE

Good little appetizer. Not well known. Exclusively French. Almost identical to American tartar sauce.

2 celery roots
2 cups mayonnaise
1/2 cup fine chopped dill pickles
2 T capers, drained
1 T mustard
2 T fresh chopped parsley
Option: 1 T each fresh chopped tarragon, chives and chervil,
        in addition to the parsley.

Peel and quarter the celery roots, simmer 3 minutes. Drain, cool, cut into julienne strips.

While the roots are cooling, make sauce by mixing all the remaining ingredients together. Mix still warm but never steaming céleri (sauce will become watery) into the sauce. Refrigerate at least three hours to develop flavor.

NOTE: You can reduce the recipe by using one root, one cup
       mayonnaise, etc. While it is a good idea to keep one
       root to approximately one cup mayo, quantities of
       other ingredients may be treated with more nonchalance.

GRATIN AU CHOU-FLEUR

Crunchy on top, a treat in cold weather, good choice for pot luck suppers.

1 LARGE head cauliflower
4 T butter
4 T flour
1 cup milk
1 cup light cream
Salt and pepper to taste
1/2 cup chopped or grated Swiss cheese
Parmesan cheese to taste

Break cauliflower into florets. Bring a pot of water to a boil, add cauliflower, let water return to a boil, count to five. Quickly drain, plunge veggies into a pot of cold water that you have ready in the sink. Count to ten, drain again.

Heat milk and cream together. Make a roux with the butter and flour; stir in hot liquid. When sauce has thickened — within minutes if the liquid is hot and you add it slowly and stir passionately — remove from heat. Stir in seasonings and Swiss cheese and stir until you cannot see the cheese. Arrange cauliflower in one layer in a buttered shallow baking dish. Pour sauce over top, sprinkle with Parmesan cheese.

Bake in a preheated 350° oven 30 minutes or until heated through and tipped with golden brown. Increase heat to 425° for the last 10 minutes or run dish under broiler for the *gratin*, or thin brown crust.

CORN SCRAPED

Cook corn on the cob. Cool, scrape off kernels. (You may also use frozen or canned corn kernels.) Drizzle with a bit of olive oil, sprinkle with a touch of fresh snipped cilantro or mint. Sauté in olive oil for 1 minute.

EGGPLANT PARMIGIANA

means a baking pan layered with eggplant, tomato sauce (or tomatoes), mozzarella and Parmesan cheeses.

Two 1 or 2 lb eggplants, peeled, cut into slices, drained *
2 to 3 cups tomato sauce with herbs
1/2 to 1 lb mozzarella, coarsely grated
1 cup grated Parmesan (roughly one 5 oz package)
Corn or olive oil for cooking
Butter for the sake of presentation

OPTION: When fresh ripe juicy field tomatoes are in season, use
            several thinly sliced ones instead of tomato sauce. Sprinkle
            with herbs. (Tomatoes are kissing cousins to basil and
            oregano but take to other herbs with aplomb.)

While eggplant slices drain, grate the mozzarella, grate the Parmesan, grease an about 9 x 13 inch baking pan. Pat the eggplant dry, sauté in hot oil, turning once and adding more oil as needed — you'll use about 1/4 cup in all. As each batch browns, transfer to paper towels. After one sheet of toweling is filled up, layer another one on top, and so on.

Now for the real layers: since your goal is to make two layers of egg-plant/tomato sauce/mozzarella, in addition to a "lid" of eggplant/Parme-san, begin by arranging one-third of the eggplant slices over the bottom of the pan. Add half the tomato sauce (or sliced juicy tomatoes and herbs), half the mozzarella and one-third of the Parmesan.

Do a second layer: one-third eggplant, remaining sauce and mozzarella, one-third Parmesan. Dot with 2 of 3 T butter. Bake in a preheated 400° for 35 minutes or until crisp and golden.

* See *The Eggplant Has a Secret*, page 5.

DIVORCE CASSEROLE

7 onions
2 T butter for the sauté
Salt and pepper
8½ oz jar dried tomatoes
2 or 3 slices peasant bread
2 T fresh grated Parmesan cheese
2 T butter for the topping

Peel or chop onions. This will make you cry. Sauté in butter for 5 minutes and season with salt and pepper to taste.

Off heat, stir in the dried tomatoes, including their marinade.

Turn into an oiled casserole. Cut and tear bread (rip up with a vengeance), with or without crusts, into enough crummy crumbs to cover the surface of the onion mix. Sprinkle with Parmesan and dot with butter. Bake in a preheated 350° oven 45 minutes.

THE POTATO, CARROT AND ONION CLUB

These three classic root vegetables make the world go round because they go together as no others do.

Peel equal amounts of potatoes and carrots and a slightly smaller amount of onions. Chop into chunks. Bring to a boil and simmer, covered, 15 minutes or until tender. Drain, toss with butter, salt and pepper.

You can also mash everything together. Peas or turnips make an OK addition, but this is a little like fixing something when it isn't broke.

The dish may be made potluck-show-off by baking: pile the cooked and buttered ensemble into a greased casserole dish and cover lightly with torn buttered bread crumbs and, if you like, the merest touch of grated Parmesan. Bake at 350° for 20 minutes or until the surface is crisp and crunchy.

LEMON NEW POTATOES

Simmer small new potatoes in their lovely red jackets for 10 minutes or until tender — depends on their size. Drain, toss with butter, lemon zest, salt, pepper, and fresh minced parsley or dill.

POMMES DE TERRE DAUPHINOISE

6 cups thinly sliced peeled potatoes
1 cup milk
1 cup heavy cream
3 cloves garlic, chopped
1/2 cup grated Swiss cheese
2 T butter

Scald milk and cream with garlic. Make three layers of potatoes in a buttered shallow baking dish and sprinkle each layer with salt, pepper, Swiss cheese.

Add the hot liquid, which should come almost to the surface of the potatoes. (It will rise bubbling to the top of the potatoes during the baking process.) Dot with butter. Bake in a preheated 350° oven 30 minutes or until golden brown.

SCALLOPED POTATOES
(American Dauphinoise)

4 cups thinly sliced peeled potatoes
1 onion, chopped
2 T flour
Salt and pepper to taste
2 T butter
1 1/2 cups hot milk
Paprika

Arrange three or four layers in a greased baking dish — one each of potatoes, onion, a mix of flour, salt and pepper, and butter. Add layers until everything is used, ending with butter. Pour milk over surface. Sprinkle with paprika to taste. Bake, covered, 45 minutes in a preheated 350° oven. Uncover, bake 20 minutes longer.

HOT PUNGENT POTATO SALAD

5 large potatoes, peeled and sliced thin
1/4 lb bacon, chopped
1 onion, chopped
Handful of minced parsley
Salt and pepper to taste
1/4 cup (4 T) vinegar
2 T sugar

Bring potato slices to a boil, cover, simmer 3 or 4 minutes or until barely tender. Drain. Sauté bacon and onion together, giving bacon a head start of five minutes. Pour bacon, onion, and drippings over warm, not steaming, potatoes, and toss gently. Taste for saltiness (the bacon is extremely salty) before adding parsley, salt and pepper. Cook vinegar, sugar, and 2 T water together for two minutes. Pour over potatoes, toss gently.

RATATOUILLE (ra-ta-TU-IE)

The ultimate dish from Provence for using late summer garden produce.

4 T olive oil
3 cloves garlic, chopped
3 onions, sliced
3 green peppers, sliced
1 eggplant, peeled & sliced
2 small zucchini, sliced
5 tomatoes, peeled & sliced
Salt and pepper

Over a low heat, cook garlic in 2 T of the olive oil. Do not let it burn. Add remaining vegetables in layers, seasoning each with salt and pepper. Drizzle about two more T oil over top. Cover, cook over very low heat for one hour. Stir gently from time to time to mix the layers and distribute the fragrance.

Uncover, turn up heat for a final 10 minutes to thicken the sauce the tomatoes have made. Serve hot, cold, or reheated, with a stick of French bread to mop up the goo.

NOTE: You may sauté the onion and green pepper with the garlic, add herbs, more or less of any vegetable, and you may want to chop, not slice. You don't have to layer. The only rule is to indulge passionately in the ritual.

TEMPURA

is a Japanese dish that consists of raw vegetable pieces turned into lacy confection via deep frying in gossamer batter. As with pancakes, tempura requires the cook to do the work at the last minute. The best way to handle the situation is 1) Don't be frazzled: have table set, salad ready, and vegetables sliced and ready before you heat the oil; and 2) Don't prepare tempura for more than two or three persons including yourself.

BUT OH HOW SUMPTUOUS IT IS AND WHAT LOVELY STUFF ON EVERY PLATE.

Vegetables: green pepper strips, broccoli florets, cauliflower florets, diagonally sliced asparagus spears, slices or whole mushrooms, whole slender green beans, onion rings, diagonally sliced zucchini and carrots, sweet potato slices, whole sugar snap peas, and so on and so on. The choice is yours, and you need choose only three or four.

Dip each variety of vegetable, which you have cut into uniform pieces for uniform cooking, in batter, then into a pot of corn oil (two inches or more deep) heated to hot but not smoking (320° to 350°). The batter will puff and turn faintly golden and the color of each item will glow through its transparent covering.

Cook each veggie two to five minutes, depending on density of variety and size of cut. Cook shrimp (shelled) — or chunks of flounder, haddock or cod — one minute. Drain everything on paper towels.

As you arrange the crisp delicacies on each plate, imagine that you are mounting an exhibition at an outré gallery. Serve with rice and tamari soy sauce.

For the batter, mix together:

2 cups flour
2 cups + 2 T water
2 eggs, beaten
Salt to taste (use at least 1/2 t)

SALAD

CREATIVE THINKING AND SALADS

RAW VEGGIE SALAD

Toss warm cauliflower florets (barely cooked, 1 to 1½ minutes) with raw red pepper and carrot strips and a dash of cooked bulgur wheat (see page 92 for cooking time). The color combination is a pleasure. As an option, add red onion rings, minced scallions, or cut-up sweet pickles. Season with salt and pepper, toss with dressing, refrigerate. Sprinkle each serving with a chopped fresh herb of choice.

PASTA SALAD

Toss cooked pasta of any variety with chopped anchovies, chopped artichoke hearts, red or green pepper strips, black or green olives, raw broccoli florets, scallions (including some of the green tops, finely minced). Include oil from the tin of anchovies, also some of the marinade from the jar of artichoke hearts (if you use marinated ones) in the dressing. Season with salt and pepper.

SHELLFISH SALAD

Arrange crisp leaves of Boston lettuce on a plate for a compartmental design — roughly, three nests. Place a handful of crabmeat or cooked chilled shrimp in one section and half an avocado, thinly sliced and holding its shape* in another. Arrange hard boiled egg wedges and 2 or 3 extremely thin rings of red onion in the third. Season with salt and pepper to taste and garnish with a sprig of fresh herb (or chop and sprinkle it over your design). Serve dressing on the side in a small old-fashioned pitcher.

* Put avocado-half on lettuce cut side down. Slice through while holding in place.

TABOULE

Taboule comes from Lebanon and in the West is also spelled tabbouleh and tabouli. It is tart on the tongue and colorful to the eye. The person who does not like it does not exist.

1/2 cup bulgur wheat
2 or 3 juicy red garden fresh tomatoes in bite size pieces
1 cup minced parsley
1/2 cup sliced scallions
2 cloves garlic, chopped
1/2 cup fresh lemon juice
1/2 cup olive oil
3 packed T or more fresh chopped mint
Salt and pepper to taste

Mix everything and marinate in the fridge at least 6 hours. Turn into a glass bowl, serve. May also be mounded onto a bed of lettuce.

EMERGENCY SALAD

At 10:30 AM on a superb August day, the camp kitchen's oversized ovens broke down. Although emergency repair service arrived within the hour, it was too late to save the lunch menu, which depended on the use of all eight ovens. To state that 200 campers and counselors who arise at dawn to sail, play tennis, build kayaks, work in the farm garden and study the environment on 300 acres are hungry at noon is a major understatement.

After a moment of collective panic the chef marched our small kitchen crew like a parade into the walk-in (refrigerator room). We emerged chilled and triumphant with armloads of farm-fresh vegetables, cold cuts and, leftover from that morning's breakfast, hard boiled eggs and fresh pineapple chunks.

Working rapidly to meet the noon deadline we made lettuce beds on 20 oversized platters. Atop each we created a mound composed of the following:

   Sliced raw carrots
   Sliced pepperoni

Sliced raw red onions
Strips of cold cuts
Sliced raw mushrooms
Whole black pitted olives
Sliced raw broccoli
Wedges of hard-boiled egg
Cold cooked chick peas
Chunks of pineapple

For more than 40 young vegetarians we left several platters free of the pepperoni and cold cuts.

On the side we prepared 20 bowls of creamy dressing (mayonnaise mixed with lemon juice and Parmesan cheese) and 20 bowls of mixed grated cheddar and Provolone cheese. We served it with 20 baskets of blueberry muffins that fit into the narrow compartments of the pizza oven.

Take it from a camp cook, emergency salad is fated for success. But don't forget the hot (FRESH WILD MAINE) blueberry muffins, page 116.

EARLY 20TH CENTURY CAESAR SALAD

Due to the risks of infection from uncooked or undercooked eggs, the original version of Caesar Salad has been banished from this page.

Though the American Egg Board has published a Cooked Creamy Caesar-Style Dressing, it cannot be compared to the ritual of tossing a madly intoxicating combination of romaine lettuce with a rich dressing*, which you then added a beaten egg to, tossed a second time until every green leaf sparkled and, as if that were not excitement enough, to which you then added freshly sautéed croutons and . . . tossed again.

READ ABOUT THE RISKS OF UNCOOKED EGGS ON PAGE 185.

* 1 minced clove garlic, ½ cup olive oil, ¼ cup lemon juice, ½ cup crumbled blue cheese, a dash of Tabasco, salt and pepper to taste, 1 T mustard.

LATE 20TH CENTURY CAESAR SALAD

This version (minus the egg, plus chicken or seafood) started showing up in the 1980s. It is a staple on the menu at Slate's in the riverside village of Hallowell, which is a must for aficionados of small restaurants and antique shops. The following is not Slate's recipe (as far as I know), but it's a good one.

Tear romaine and/or Boston lettuce leaves. Toss with an oil and lemon juice dressing.

Add the following and toss again:

>Cooked shrimp or leftover chicken cut into bite size
>Drained anchovy fillets*
>Crumbled blue cheese (just enough to tantalize)
>Grated Parmesan cheese (even less)
>OPTION: Crisp bacon pieces

Add croutons, salt and pepper and toss for the third time, bearing in mind that the anchovies have already added salt to the salad.

* Discard oil in tin or use it in making the dressing.

SALADE NIÇOISE

Like certain other French specialties — *pommes frites*, *croissants*, *café au lait*, *Brie* — the original taste can be imitated but never equaled. Brilliantly delicious on a summer day.

Use small, whole red new potatoes in the skin (if you can't find any, use thinly sliced potatoes of another variety). Slice or wedge the eggs — or grate them. (Niçoise gets your creative juices flowing.) Use long, slender, whole green beans — or beans sliced in half lengthwise. Toss beans with the other ingredients — or arrange them on top in a starburst. Be equally serendipitous with the tomatoes.

Think Provence: blazing sun, olive trees, the Matisse chapel, fishing boats, tile roofs, crooked streets, sidewalk cafés, flowers on window ledges, flowers in shops, flowers in fields. Niçoise territory.

The amounts of the ingredients may be manipulated.

1/2 lb small new potatoes
1/2 lb very fresh slender green beans
1/2 lb fresh tuna, grilled, or 6 to 8 oz canned, drained
1/2 red onion, sliced elegantly thin
2 hard boiled eggs, sliced or wedged
6 to 8 oil cured black olives
2 fresh juicy tomatoes, sliced or wedged
6 anchovies
2 t capers
Boston lettuce leaves to line plates
2 T each chopped fresh tarragon & parsley

AHEAD OF TIME

Cook potatoes and, in a separate pot, steam beans until barely done —
they beg to retain crunch. Drain beans, plunge into cold water (this will
seal the bright green color). Dry thoroughly. Toss potatoes and beans
separately with an oil and vinegar dressing, refrigerate (separately) for
several hours or overnight. (You might also toss potatoes with mayonnaise with a good douse of lemon juice mixed in. The dressing does not
have to be identical to that of the beans.)

Before serving, gather ingredients, arrange in a symmetrical pattern on
two or three plates which you have lined with leaves of Boston. Drizzle
on a four-to-one olive oil-lemon juice dressing or serve it in a small pitcher
on the side. Or you may toss the works together. Whatever form you
present, sprinkle herbs over the top.

LEMON CARROT SALAD

Peel and grate carrots. Toss with mayonnaise into which you have mixed
fresh lemon juice (four parts mayo to one part lemon juice). Stir in salt
and pepper and a touch of grated onion. Do not add raisins. (Who
started the raisins-in-carrot-salad epidemic?) Sprinkle with a freshly
snipped herb — thyme, flower heads and all, would be just right.

AVOCADO SALAD FOR TWO

Do not peel but cut an avocado in half lengthwise. Place in two small
bowls. Fill cavities 3/4 full with olive oil. Add fresh lemon juice to rim and
let it spill over. Sprinkle with salt and pepper to taste.

LENTIL SALAD

Cook lentils (see chart on page 92) and drain well. While still warm but with no traces of steam left toss gently with chopped scallions and basic dressing or a lemon-doctored mayonnaise. Sprinkle with a fresh minced herb.

TUNA ARTICHOKE SALAD

Mix two 6 oz cans tuna, drained and fork flaked, with one 16 oz can artichoke hearts, drained and chopped, and 1/4 cup chopped black olives. Toss with 1/3 cup mayonnaise mixed with lemon juice from — it depends on how lemony you like the dressing — a half or a whole lemon. Add salt and pepper and a fresh herb to taste.

CRISP AUTUMN HARVEST SALAD

Carrots
Beets
Cabbage
Apple chunks, peeled
Walnuts, chopped
Lettuce

Grate raw carrots, beets, and cabbage. Toss with a handful of apples and walnuts. Toss again with an oil and vinegar dressing. Serve on a bed of greens.

CUCUMBER SALAD MOUSSE

This is an artifact from an era when ladies not women (dangerous concept) gathered for luncheon not lunch. The spread might consist of ersatz salads and processed foods from recipes inspired by post WW II tech and worked up in new "test kitchens". Trimmings included such fare as tiny (ladylike) marshmallows and maraschino cherries. How could women stand it? Some of them couldn't. (Ask my mom.)

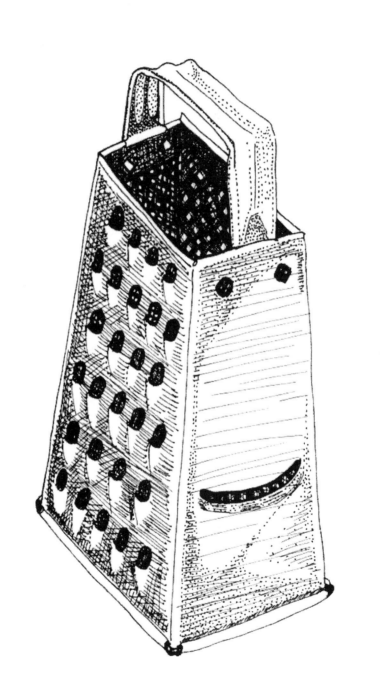

Cucumber salad mousse is neither salad nor mousse. It's a mutant. On the plus side, the frosty mint color cools the psyche on a hot summer day. The taste appeals, the sweet tooth profits and, for the cook of the day, the ritual of assembly is therapeutic.

Once every seven years, serve at lunch(eon).

One 3 oz box lime flavored gelatin dessert
1 cup grated cucumber, firmly packed
2 T grated onion
1/2 cup mayonnaise
1 cup plain yogurt
Flower blossoms
Thin slices of lime
Fresh mint leaves

Dissolve gelatin dessert in 3/4 cup boiling water in a bowl. Refrigerate until slightly thickened, 12 to 15 minutes.

Grate cucumbers. (If they are small and garden fresh, do not peel. Otherwise do.) Mix gratings, which don't have to be bone dry but should not look like a flood, with onion, mayonnaise and yogurt.

Stir into gelatin. (If mix has started to jell on bottom, scrape up bits and stir into the whole. It will give the mousse disarming green flecks.) Turn into a 4 cup ring mold that has been rinsed with water. Refrigerate overnight or for at least 6 hours.

Unmold onto a rinsed platter. Fill center with flower blossoms. Tuck thin slices of lime or small mint leaves around the base of the mold or sprinkle minced mint leaves over the top.

SOUPS

MAKE SOUP

Concocting soup is like building sand castles on the beach: a dreamy activity. On top of which you get *soup*. In an ideal world you go for a walk while the soup cooks, the better to return and open the door to the enchanting aroma of herbs on the simmer.

MECHANICS: You make soup with a base of 1) water, 2) broth, 3) a mix of water and broth, or 4) any of the above mixed with milk or cream. The first option, water, is the one the villagers use in the children's story, *Stone Soup*, which reveals how sharing brings happiness.

The second option, broth, is the one most recipes call for because the flavor cooks up into a soup that gives pleasure the minute the pot leaves the fire. By comparison, water-based soup can be bland despite its seasonings until it spends an overnight in the fridge to uncork its mysterious ecstasies. And yet . . . no one would call seafood chowder (page 36) bland, though not a drop of broth does it have to its name.

The medicinal properties of chicken broth in soup are legendary. But beware heavy-handed sodium in some canned versions. You can put a salty broth in its place by diluting with water, or you can buy the low-sodium version. When I use a recipe that calls for four cups of chicken broth, I frequently use two cups of water and two of canned broth, even three cups of water and one of broth.

Cubes that dissolve in boiling water make the broth of last resort — soup tastes like a chemical factory.

The addition of cream to a soup bestows unspeakable enchantment.

BEANS: Lentil and other soups composed of more beans than anything else thicken as they soak, cook and refrigerate. Those beans just keep drinking liquid and growing fatter and fatter. If your soup solidifies into cement, thin with water or broth.

MISO:	This is a soybean product and delightful stuff when stirred into soup. It's so health-giving that some people say you should sip miso soup every morning. (After the infamous bombing of Hiroshima, one hospital that served miso daily to all its patients observed a lower incidence of radiation sickness and death than at other hospitals and in the population at large.*)

Miso exerts its own flavor and is salty — so don't salt until after you've tasted. On the plus side, miso is inarguably health-giving and adds zip to a water-based soup. If in doubt, go to a natural foods store and ask questions and — off you sail. Experimenting with new ways of thinking. Don't add miso to soup until just after you've removed it from the heat. Miso is not happy being cooked.

* *Staying Healthy With the Seasons*, Elson M. Haas, M.D.

CHICKEN BROTH

Cook chicken neck, giblets and any leftover bones or scraps (but not the liver) in water with chopped potatoes, onions, celery (with leaves, if any) and several teaspoons of dried herbs — bay leaf and thyme are good traditional choices, but you should do as you like. Use 2 or 3 cups water for each one cup of chopped vegetables. Stay away from the strong tastes of such items as cabbage, broccoli and rosemary. They can make themselves more important than is good for the community pot.

Simmer everything, partially covered, for an hour or more. Skim surface as necessary and add salt and pepper to taste. The liquid will reduce, concentrating the flavor. Cool, strain. Discard chicken and veggie pieces. Refrigerate or freeze.

VEGGIE BROTH

Follow above instructions but omit chicken.

CAPE PORPOISE SEAFOOD CHOWDER

When Sarah gave me this recipe it had canned evaporated milk in the lineup. I protested the "mistake" in her otherwise wildly delicious chowder and pointed out that fresh milk and cream were the only products to use. She remained firm in *her* opinion: evaporated milk.

The "cracklins" in the recipe bear witness to Sarah's southern origins. She moved – in her new husband's sailboat – from West Virginia to the coast of Maine 40 years ago. He had built the boat in his grandfather's Indiana barn and knocked down the wall to remove it. Towed it to Ohio, set sail on Lake Erie, dropped anchor in Virginia, collected Sarah inland, and continued to Cape Porpoise, where they've lived, sailing the summers away, ever since.

1/2 lb salt pork, chopped
2 onions, chopped
2 T butter
6 potatoes, peeled and chopped bite size
2 cups water
Salt and pepper to taste
1 lb or more chopped haddock, scrod, or flounder fillets,
1 cup heavy cream mixed with 1 cup milk
Fresh parsley
OPTION: Handful shelled cooked shrimp

Cover salt pork with water, bring to a boil, simmer three minutes, drain. Fry (do not grease skillet) over medium heat until browned and crisp, about 15 minutes. Drain on paper towels, set aside.

Sauté onions in butter. Add potatoes and stir for two minutes. Take pot briefly off heat, add water, salt and pepper (be judicious with the salt because the salt pork is loaded with it). Bring to a boil, simmer 10 minutes or until potatoes are tender. Add seafood, return to a boil, simmer 5 minutes longer. Stir in milk-cream mix, heat for several minutes but do boil.

Serve salt pork "cracklins" on the side or scatter over each bowl of steaming chowder.

Sprinkle minced parsley over each serving.

CUBAN BLACK BEAN SOUP

As the touch of black in an Amish quilt gives meaning to the riot of color, the addition of black beans to stir-fries or salads creates vigor of design and color. As for black bean soup, it leads a piquant life of its own.

1 cup black beans
5 cups broth, or a 50/50 broth-water mix
2 T olive oil
2 or 3 stalks celery, chopped, including leaves
1 onion, chopped
1/4 cup fresh lemon juice
1 T mustard
1 t cumin
1 t chili powder
1 t oregano
Salt to taste
Thin slices lemon and hard boiled egg

Soak beans overnight. Discard soaking water and add broth. Bring to a boil and simmer, covered, 1 ½ hours.

Sauté celery and onion in oil. Add to beans. Stir in lemon juice, mustard, spices and salt. Return to a boil, cover, simmer 10 minutes. Cool to room temperature, purée in blender or processor, reheat 24 to 48 hours later.

OPTION: When you reheat, stir in a splash of sherry.

GARNISH: Float thin slices of lemon and egg atop each bowl.

BETTER BUTTERNUT BISQUE

1 butternut squash
2 T butter
1 onion, chopped
1 T curry powder
2 or 3 carrots, chopped
1 ½ cups broth or a broth/water mix
1 potato, peeled and chopped
1 apple, peeled, cored and chopped
1 cup light cream or milk

Chop squash into chunks, scrape out seeds. Cover with water, bring to a boil and simmer, covered, 5-10 minutes or until tender when pierced with a fork. Drain, rinse with cold water, let cool.

Cook onion, carrots, potato and apple in butter in a large heavy pot for 5 minutes. Off heat, stir in curry powder and broth or broth-water mix. Bring to a boil and simmer, covered, 20 minutes.

Slice off rind of squash and add to pot. Add salt and pepper. Cool slightly, whir in a blender or processor (if you haven't got tech, hand-mash the veggies and don't worry about lumps, which add personality). Just before serving, stir in cream and reheat but do not boil. Garnish each serving with a dollop of sour cream and a scattering of a fresh herb of choice.

CORN CHOWDER

Immensely delicious towards the *end* of that time of year when local farmers sell fresh corn. At the *beginning* of the harvest your sensuality is more richly rewarded by eating corn on the cob and getting butter on your fingers.

2 T butter
2 stalks celery, sliced
2 onions, chopped into bite size
2 potatoes, chopped into bite size
1 to 1 ½ cups water
4 cups kernels scraped off cooked corn on the cob
2 cups half and half, milk, light cream, or a mix
Fresh parsley
Crisply cooked diced bacon

Cook celery and onions gently in butter in a large pot for 3 minutes. Add potatoes, stir for another minute. Stir in salt and pepper to taste. Add water barely to cover, bring to a boil, simmer, covered, 15 minutes or until potato pieces are tender. Cut corn off cobs, add to the pot. When the water returns to a boil, turn again to a simmer, cover, and cook 5 minutes.

While it cooks, put some parsley and bacon pieces into each soup bowl. Ladle in the soup for a Yankee feast.

FENNEL SOUP

Fennel is the bulbous vegetable that tastes like anise (licorice).

2 onions chopped into bite size
2 T butter
1 fennel bulb chopped into bite size
2 potatoes chopped into bite size
3 to 4 cups chicken broth
Juice of 1 lime
Finely chopped fennel stalks + 2 t butter
Finely chopped fennel ferns

Sauté onions in butter. Add bulb pieces and continue to sauté. Add potatoes, sauté for 2 minutes. Add broth and lime juice, bring to a boil, cover, simmer 10-15 minutes or until potatoes are cooked through. Cool slightly.

Purée in a blender or processor, reheat. Sauté a bit of the stalk in butter, seasoning with salt and pepper. Garnish each serving with fennel stalks and misty blue-green ferns.

SCOTCH BROTH

(what a delicious thing to do with leftover leg of lamb)

1 meaty lamb bone
Brothmakers (chunks of unpeeled onion, unpeeled carrots, celery with leaves)
Salt and pepper
1 T dried thyme
3 quarts water
1/2 cup barley
1 cup each diced, peeled carrots, celery and onion
Fresh chopped parsley
OPTION: 1 cup diced, peeled turnip

Simmer bone, unpeeled veggies, salt, pepper and thyme in water in a covered pot for two hours. Strain into a large pot, discarding vegetables. Remove excess meat from bone, chop and refrigerate. Discard bone. Refrigerate broth overnight.

Remove congealed fat from surface of broth. Add barley, cover, bring to a boil, simmer 30 minutes. Add diced, peeled vegetables, return to a boil, cover, simmer 15 minutes. Add reserved bits of meat. Scatter parsley over each serving.

NOTE: If you omit the bone from the soup greens, you are cooking vegetable broth that may be added to just about any soup you wish to make.

CHUNKY CREAMY VEGGIE SOUP

In the middle of a Maine winter, when shutters bang and windows rattle, this fuels your furnace.

5 carrots, chopped
5 potatoes, chopped
3 celery stalks, chopped
2 onions, chopped
4 T butter
4 T flour
1 cup light cream
2 to 3 cups canned tomatoes, with juice
Fresh dill

Cover vegetables with 4 cups water, bring to a boil, cover, simmer 20 to 30 minutes or until tender. Drain water into a bowl. Make a roux (see Roux Who, page 50) with butter and flour and slowly stir in 3 cups of the cooking water. Cook and stir until slightly thickened. Season with salt, pepper, and an herb of your choice.

Mash vegetables roughly with an old-fashioned potato masher. You want to leave some chunks intact. Chop tomatoes if they need it to be bite size and, using some of their liquid (use your discretion for a thinner or thicker soup), add to the pot. Stir in the sauce. Cool to room temperature, refrigerate to develop flavor.

At serving time, add cream and reheat. Scatter dill over each bowl of hot, steaming, rib-sticking soup. OR: scatter dill into bottom of every bowl, ladle soup over it. The scene carries more panache if the chef does this in front of everyone.

WINTER ROOT SOUP

If this doesn't stick to the ribs nothing will. The recipe comes from Bath's Truffles Café, an irresistible hole-in-the-wall where chef owner Ellen greets locals and strangers alike with warmth and cheer.

1 large Spanish onion	1 rutabaga
4 carrots	3 potatoes
3 large stalks celery	2 sweet potatoes
3 T olive oil	2 quarts water
1 t salt	2 cups lentils
1/2 t crushed red pepper flakes	4 T tomato paste
3 cloves garlic, chopped	1 bay leaf
4 parsnips	1/2 cup sliced scallions

Peel/chop onion, carrots and celery in bite size pieces and sauté in the olive oil in a seriously roomy stock pot 30 minutes, stirring often. Add salt, red pepper flakes and garlic, sauté 5 more minutes, stirring once or twice. Peel/chop parsnips, rutabaga, potatoes and sweet potatoes. Add to pot and stir around for 45 seconds.

Add water, lentils (rinsed for stones), tomato paste, and bay leaf. Bring to a boil, stirring to make sure nothing sticks to the bottom. Add more water if you think the pot is needy. Boil, uncovered, 2 minutes, reduce heat to a simmer and stir continuously for another 2 or 3 minutes. Cover and simmer 45 to 60 minutes or until lentils are cooked through. Remove bay leaf.

Adjust seasoning with salt and red pepper flakes, toss scallions onto the top of each serving.

ONION SOUP

This is labor intensive.

4 onions, sliced
4 T butter
2 T flour
4 cups hot chicken or vegetable broth
French bread
Grated Parmesan cheese
Sour cream and chopped parsley

Sauté onions in butter in a soup pot until translucent, about 10 minutes. Stir flour into onions. When blended, slowly add hot broth, salt and pepper to taste. Cook and stir until soup starts to boil. Cover, simmer 15 minutes.

While soup is asimmer, run French bread slices sprinkled with Parmesan under the broiler. Float a slice of toast on top of each serving.

OPTION: Place untoasted slices atop each serving in ovenproof soup crocks and broil everything at once. Or use more than one slice per crock for a wall-to-wall broiled cheese-on-toast effect. SERVE SMALL DISHES OF SOUR CREAM AND PARSLEY ON THE SIDE.

A BASIC SPLIT PEA (OR LENTIL) SOUP FORMULA

This recipe makes such a thick soup that a wit at my table once said, "Hey, look! My spoon stands up in my soup."

2 onions
2 stalks celery
2 carrots
2 potatoes
1 cup split peas OR lentils
5 cups chicken or vegetable broth
1 T dried herb of choice
1 bay leaf

Peel such vegetables as you feel need it, chop into bite-size, sauté in 2 T olive oil in a large heavy pot. Off heat, add beans of choice, the liquid and the herbs. Season to taste with salt and pepper. Bring to a boil, cover, simmer 45 minutes. Turn off heat but do not remove cover. After soup has come to room temperature, refrigerate overnight to develop flavor. Reheat at serving time. Fish out bay leaf, discard.

OPTION: Garnish each serving with croutons.

NOTE: Many cooks add pieces of cooked ham to split peas or add a ham bone to the soup as it cooks. (Split peas and ham have a particular regard for each other.)

AFTER YOU HAVE BECOME FAMILIAR with the basic formula you will start adding the likes of spinach, chopped tomatoes or tomato sauce, dried mint, hot chiles, lime juice, and so on. Lentil or split pea soup is also tasty cooked with nothing more than onions, salt and pepper (possibly a potato to give it body).

VICHYSSOISE
(cold soup for hot summer)

1 onion, peeled and sliced
4 to 5 leeks, peeled, cleaned and sliced*
2 T butter
5 to 6 potatoes, peeled and sliced
4 cups chicken or veggie broth
Salt and pepper to taste
2 cups milk
2 cups heavy or light cream
Fresh chives

In a soup pot, sauté onion and leek slices in the butter for several minutes. Stir in potato slices for another minute. Pull pot off heat to add broth. Stir in salt and pepper, return to heat, bring to a boil. Turn to a simmer and cook, covered, 20 minutes. Let cool.

Purée in blender or processor in batches — or do it the way the French once did: press the vegetables through a sieve by hand. Refrigerate. *Chill thoroughly.* Stir in milk and cream. Snip fresh chives over each serving.

NOTE: Fresh snipped parsley or tarragon would also make an attractive garnish. But chives carry on the onion family theme, and it's a fine tradition to honor.

* See page 6 for cleaning leeks.

OYSTER STEW FOR TWO

Eat it at the 19th century Oyster Bar in Grand Central Terminal before you catch the 21st century train that zips you to Maine at 150 MPH.

1 pint oysters with liquid
2 T butter
2 T chili sauce
2 t Worcestershire
Juice of one lemon
1/2 cup light cream
Oyster crackers

Place oysters, butter, chili sauce, Worcestershire and lemon juice in a pot. Cook briskly for a minute, stirring constantly. Add cream. When it comes almost to a boil, pour into warmed bowls. Slurp it up with oyster crackers and a good white wine.

MONHEGAN ISLAND GAZPACHO

The ingredients are a giveaway that this is a late summer specialty.

4 slices rough wholegrain bread in pieces
4 cloves garlic, chopped
Juice of 1 lemon
1 quart (4 cups) good quality tomato juice
About 10 ripe luscious garden fresh tomatoes, peeled and chopped
1 garden fresh onion, chopped, or 1/2 cup chopped scallions
5 small garden fresh cucumbers, peeled and chopped
2 garden fresh green peppers, chopped
3 T vinegar
4 T olive oil
Salt and pepper to taste
Croutons (page 119)
Parsley for garnish

In a blender or processor whir up bread (crust optional), garlic, lemon juice, and one cup of the tomato juice. Turn into a large bowl, add remaining ingredients except croutons and parsley. Be wise in the amount of tomato juice you add — if the tomatoes you're working with are big juicy ones, really ripe, you may want to use less than three full cups of juice. Now turn everything back into the machine and do some more whirring — not too much. The texture of gazpacho has more appeal when it is slightly rough rather than silky smooth.

Refrigerate overnight or for at least six hours so that the flavors assert themselves. Garnish each serving with several croutons and, if you wish, a beautiful, fresh, delicious sprig of parsley.

LEEK AND POTATO SOUP

This is the winter version of vichyssoise.

3 T butter
1 onion
5 leeks
6 potatoes
3 cups water
Salt and pepper
1 cup heavy cream
1 cup milk
Fresh parsley
Fresh chives, if you can find them

Peel, chop veggies into bite size pieces. (Be sure to clean the leeks of all grit (page 6.) Sauté onion and leeks in butter. Add potatoes, stir for a few minutes. Add water, salt and pepper to taste, bring to a boil, cover, simmer 20 minutes. Stir in cream and milk. Reheat but do not boil.

Garnish with snipped parsley and chives and grated pepper.

KATUSNIAK
(Hungarian sauerkraut soup)

1 onion, chopped
1 T butter
1 T flour
2 cups hot chicken broth
1 T caraway seeds
3 to 4 cups chopped cabbage
1/2 lb sauerkraut
1/4 to 1/2 lb bacon, cooked and chopped
2 cups light cream

Sauté onion in butter. Make a roux by stirring in flour. After a minute, slowly stir in hot broth. When well blended and slightly thickened, add caraway seeds, cabbage, sauerkraut. Bring to a boil, cover, simmer 15 minutes or until cabbage is tender.

Off heat, stir in bacon. If you plan to eat soon, add cream and heat but do not boil. Otherwise, cool soup to room temperature, place in fridge for up to three days, add cream when you reheat.

Katusniak offers better flavor every time you refrigerate and reheat it.

"SOUL" SOUP

1 onion, chopped
3 T butter
3 T flour mixed with 2 t curry powder
One 8 oz bottle clam juice mixed with 1 cup water, heated
1 cup diced tomatoes, with liquid
A slurp of white wine — one third cup, more or less
1 lb sole filets cut bite size
Fresh cilantro

Make sauce: Sauté onion in butter, stir in flour/curry. When blended, stir in hot clam juice/water. Stir and heat until thickened.

Off heat, add tomatoes. Add wine. Add pepper to taste. (At this point, if time allows, cook for several minutes to slightly reduce the liquid, concentrate the flavors) Add pieces of fish. Bring to a boil, stirring once or twice. Cover, simmer 1 minute. Let rest for another minute or two. Serve in warmed bowls garnished with minced cilantro.

NOTE: You may substitute flounder, halibut, or scrod.

CREAM OF GINGER CARROT SOUP TO SERVE TEN

This soup is garnish heaven and tastes like heaven too. It is the most fanciful take of all on the potato, carrot and onion club (page 19).

6 T butter	4 cups chicken broth
2 onions, chopped	Salt and pepper to taste
6 cups sliced carrots	2 T grated ginger root
2 cups chopped potatoes	3 cups light cream

Cook onion gently in butter for 3 minutes in a very fat pot. Stir in carrots and potatoes, broth, salt, pepper, and grated ginger root. Bring to a boil, cover, simmer 15 minutes or until veggies are tender. (This is dependent on the size of the pieces you cut them into.) Cool slightly. Run through a blender or processor. Slowly stir in cream and reheat (never boil). Or refrigerate and reheat the next day.

GARNISH POTENTIAL: Scallions sliced on the diagonal, a dollop of sour cream, thin lemon or orange slices; minced parsley, cilantro, dill or mint. Scatter over surface like stardust.

CREAM OF BROCCOLI SOUP

Follow above recipe substituting a chopped head of broccoli (florets and some of the stalk) for the carrots and potatoes. Omit the ginger root, but when you reheat slowly add the juice of a lime. Garnish each serving with a dollop of sour cream.

SAUCES

ROUX WHO

Roux (rhymes with boo) is the paste that happens when you melt a tablespoon or two of butter and stir in roughly the same amount of flour. Roux is born and dies within seconds, from the time the butter and flour combine in a sweet sizzle until you start stirring in hot milk or broth. As you stir — a wire whip is best — the roux dissolves into the hot liquid, which thickens. You have just made sauce.

If the liquid you add is milk, the roux thickens into basic white sauce, which the French long ago named béchamel (bay-sha-MEL).

Embellishments such as grated cheese, mustard, egg yolk, lemon juice, or the substitution of hot broth or a milk/broth combination result in other sauces with yet more beautiful French names.

Gaunt, ragged American colonists knew all about roux, although they didn't call it that (unless they came from France). They used pan drippings from available animal fat and whole grain flour. They stirred in water, or milk or broth if they had it, and called it gravy. American gravy isn't as exquisite as French sauce, but Thanksgiving would not be the same without it.

BASIC SALAD DRESSING

"Basic" means you employ more or less — not militantly — four parts olive oil to one part vinegar or lemon juice. A more exacting rule cannot be laid down because no two olive oils or vinegar's, or cooks, have the same intensity.

4 parts good quality extra virgin olive oil
1 part fresh lemon juice or vinegar — or a mix
Salt and pepper to taste

Using a fork, whip everything together in a short, wide drinking glass or jar. Stir again before each use, keeping the container covered with plastic wrap in between. Refrigeration is not necessary.

OPTION: Garlic, mustard, horseradish, and so on — solo or in
          combination. Dressing will take on a fine garlic taste and
          fragrance if you add a garlic clove split in two or three.
          (Be sure it doesn't pour onto someone's salad. The taste
          isn't bad but it looks tacky.)

          The dynamite herb combo to sprinkle onto (preferably
          Boston) lettuce is difficult to come by: chopped fresh
          parsley, chives, chervil and tarragon.

SALAD DRESSING TERMINOLOGY: I don't say "vinaigrette" because
the word did not exist in my vocabulary until I was old enough to vote and
even then I didn't know what it meant. Jean-Pierre and I use "dressing"
and his French mother said "sauce", which with her accent came out like
"so" with an "se" on it. *Sose.*

In our house, salad means Boston lettuce sprinkled with whatever fresh
herb(s) are on hand and tossed with an oil-lemon juice dressing. Boston
is hands down the best-tasting lettuce, and it is crazy in love with lemon
juice.

HUMMUS

From Greece and North Africa, hummus has been eaten with pita bread
and olives forever and ever. In the West we eat it as A DIP — with
toasted pita bread triangles if we wish to carry on the classic theme —
or in A SANDWICH. Hummus goes with fresh sliced tomatoes like
peanut butter goes with jelly; it also strikes a tangy note with shredded
carrots, cucumber slices, and other fresh vegetables.

1 cup uncooked garbanzo beans (chick peas)
1 clove garlic, chopped
Salt to taste
Juice of 3 lemons
1/2 cup tahini
1 T paprika
OPTION: Fresh cilantro or parsley

Soak garbanzo beans overnight and make it a long night — say, 3 PM to
8 AM. Drain. Cover with fresh water, bring to a boil, simmer, covered,
2½ hours. Add more water if necessary. Drain cooking water, <u>reserve</u>.

51

Purée garbanzos with 6 T of the cooking liquid, the juice of one lemon, garlic and salt. Set aside.

Stir juice of remaining two lemons into tahini. Stir in paprika. Combine with the bean paste by hand or in batches in a processor.

If you plan to use the hummus as a dip, turn into a serving bowl, smooth with the back of a spoon, and sprinkle with additional paprika and chopped cilantro or parsley for a striking presentation. If you are using hummus as sandwich material you can skip this step, or you can stir the paprika and herb into the mixture. Refrigerate in a container with a tight-fitting cover.

TAHINI LEMON DRESSING

This affords a change of pace. Mix one part tahini with one part lemon juice. Slowly stir in up to one part water.

BABA GHANOUSH (or ghanouj)

Tart and lemony. Use as a dip with triangles of toasted pita bread.

1 or 1 ½ lb eggplant
2 cloves garlic, chopped
Juice of 2 lemons
1 T olive oil
Fresh parsley or cilantro

Prick eggplant in several places with a fork. Bake in a lightly greased pan in a preheated 400° oven until tender, 45 to 55 minutes. Cut in half lengthwise. When cool enough to handle, scoop out pulp and whir in a blender or processer with the garlic, lemon juice, olive oil, and salt and pepper to taste. You can also beat the mixture by hand.

Turn into a small serving dish, sprinkle with minced parsley or cilantro. If not using right away, cover tightly and refrigerate.

BÉCHAMEL (basic white sauce)

4 T butter
4 T flour
2 cups hot milk

Melt butter over low heat in a heavy pot. Stir in flour with a wire whisk. The mixture will froth into a roux. Stir in about 1/3 cup hot milk, stirring constantly. Gradually stir in more milk until you have used it all, continuing to stir — it takes just a few minutes — until you have a thickened sauce. Season with salt and pepper.

INCREASED FLAVOR: Add the juice of a lemon and/or a tablespoon of mustard and/or grated nutmeg or a chopped fresh herb of your choice to the thickened sauce.

SAUCE MORNAY: Stir 1/2 cup grated Parmesan or cheddar cheese into the thickened sauce.

BÉARNAISE*

The only sauce for filet mignon. Try not to substitute dried herbs for the fresh.

2 T minced scallions
1 T minced fresh tarragon
1 T minced fresh chervil
Salt and pepper to taste
1/4 cup vinegar (tarragon flavored is nice but not necessary)
4 egg yolks
2/3 cup melted butter

Simmer scallions, herbs, salt, pepper and vinegar until liquid is reduced to one or two tablespoons. Cool slightly.

One at a time beat in yolks. Place over a low heat and slowly whisk in butter until you have a sauce.

* This recipe contains egg yolks. See SPECIAL NOTE on page 185.

HOLLANDAISE*

An all-time classic, it is used traditionally as a sauce for fresh spring asparagus or Eggs Benedict, which in all its glory consists of toasted English muffin topped with hot sliced ham topped with poached egg topped with Hollandaise.

1/2 cup (1 stick) butter
3 egg yolks
1 T lemon juice — or more
Pinch salt

Melt butter. Process yolks, lemon juice and salt for 4 seconds. Using feeder tube of processor or small inner opening in blender lid, slowly pour in butter as you whir the mix. Makes about ¾ cup. Recipe doubles easily.

MAYONNAISE*

is pronounced may-o-NEZ by the French, who invented it. Mayonnaise makes a thoughtful gift, though it doesn't travel far except in a cold-pack. But it looks smooth and cool in a sparkling clean jar, tied with ribbons and sporting your hand-made label.

2 egg yolks
2 t mustard
Pinch salt
2 T fresh lemon juice
1 cup olive oil

Place yolks, mustard, salt, lemon juice and a couple of spoonfuls of olive oil in a food processor. Process smooth. With motor on, pour in the olive oil in a slow stream. As soon as the mixture emulsifies, add any options that appeal — though ITS PERFECT THE WAY IT IS. Refrigerate.

---

*   This recipe contains egg yolks. See SPECIAL NOTE on page 185.

TARTAR SAUCE

is a good partner to seafood broiled, sautéed, simmered or grilled.

1 cup mayonnaise
1 T minced fresh parsley
1 T minced fresh herb of choice
1 T minced onion or chives
2 T capers
1 small chopped sour pickle
Juice of 1 lemon

Mix, refrigerate several hours or overnight to develop flavor.

GREEN SAUCE

Drizzle over shellfish and vegetables or spread onto slices of peasant bread.

1 tin anchovy fillets
Olive oil
3 T minced fresh parsley

2 T capers
1 T mustard
Juice of 1 lemon

Pour oil from anchovy tin into a measuring cup and pour in olive oil to 1/2 cup level. Set aside. Mince anchovies, mix with remaining ingredients. Slowly stir in oil with a fork or whisk.

DABBLING IN DIPS

RAW VEGGIE DIP: Mix 1 cup mayonnaise, 4 T mustard, 2 T honey. Measure carelessly. Refrigerate several hours to develop taste, bring back to room temperature. Serve with munchies — carrot and green pepper strips, scallions, cauliflowerets, cherry tomatoes, zucchini ovals, rolled salami, cold cooked shrimp, sliced radishes . . .

GUACAMOLE: Peel, pit and mash two ripe avocados. Stir in two chopped cloves of garlic or several minced scallions. Stir in 2 T fresh lemon juice. Turn into a small serving dish and scatter chopped fresh cilantro over the surface.

CLAM DIP: This common-ordinary dip becomes food for the gods when served with common-ordinary potato chips. Knowing how to make it should be a legal requirement for everyone over six. Mix 8 oz cream cheese, 1/2 cup plain yogurt or sour cream, one 6 1/2 oz can minced clams drained of some but not all liquid, and the juice of 1 lemon.

SIZZLING HOT ARTICHOKE DIP: Chop marinated artichoke hearts (1 6 oz jar), add with their marinade to 3/4 cup each freshly grated Parmesan cheese and mayonnaise. Turn into a small greased baking dish, bake in a preheated 350° oven 10 to 15 minutes or until surface bubbles. Serve hot from the oven with thin slices of French bread.

CRÈME DE LA CRÈME

Sublime. Spoon over cooked potatoes, carrots, broccoli, meat, pasta and everything else that likes cream.

1 clove garlic, chopped
4 T butter
1 cup heavy cream
2 T lemon juice

Sauté garlic in butter in a small heavy pot. Stir in cream and heat, but do not boil. Slowly stir in lemon juice and simmer, stirring occasionally, until the cream is slightly reduced, about five minutes.

NOTE: Crème de la crème is delicious incorporated into leftover roasts. Spread half of sauce over the bottom and sides of a buttered shallow baking dish. Arrange paper thin slices of cooked meat or chicken over it in an overlapping pattern. Sprinkle with salt and pepper to taste. Spoon remaining sauce on top. Bake in a preheated 350° oven 10 minutes, or until warmed. Sprinkle with a freshly chopped herb.

PESTO

A little pesto goes a long way. Serve over or toss with pasta or steamed vegetables, or sandwich between two layers of cream cheese in a sandwich. For the record (I have not tried it), I once saw a display in a take-out emporium that laced pesto into potato salad with the usual mayonnaise dressing for a smashing red, white and green effect. (The potato skins provided the red*.)

3 packed cups chopped fresh basil leaves
1/2 cup pignoli (pine) nuts
1/2 cup olive oil (more if needed)
1/4 cup (4 T) melted butter
1/2 cup fresh-grated Parmesan cheese
2 chopped cloves garlic
Salt to taste

Mix everything together, run through a blender or food processor in batches. Makes about 1 ½ cups, which sounds like a moderate amount, but in view of pesto's intense nature is a *lot*.

* Red potatoes should be sliced with skin intact before you cook them at a simmer for 3-4 minutes for a cooked-but-crisp taste and perfect looks. (If you cook potatoes whole and then try to slice, the skin acts terrible.)

COCKTAIL SAUCE 1940

Smooth, tart, tasty. Good served with Sweltering Day Shrimp Platter (page 134) or smeared over hotdogs in buns.

In the early 20th century this sauce was used in an appetizer called shrimp cocktail — crisp little lettuce leaves lining a small stem dish into which one placed several shrimp, a topping of sauce, and a garnish of lemon wedge. It was the precursor of Sweltering Day Shrimp Platter.

1/2 cup catsup
1/2 cup chili sauce
2 T horseradish
3 T lemon juice
} Mix, cover, refrigerate.

HARD SAUCE

Cream 1/2 cup room temperature butter, gradually add one cup powdered sugar. Stir in 1 T vanilla, brandy, or rum. Chill, but be sure to remove from fridge an hour or two before serving (hard sauce should not be *hard*). Turn into a small serving bowl, dust with nutmeg, serve with apple pie.

BRANDY LEMON GLAZE

1/4 cup brandy
1/4 cup honey
1/4 cup (1/2 stick) butter at room temperature
1/4 cup fresh lemon juice

Warm brandy in skillet. Remove from heat, ignite. It will make a lovely, low blue flame. When the fire has died, gradually stir in honey. Stir in butter a tablespoon at a time. If it doesn't blend in, put the skillet over a low heat for a few seconds until it does. Stir in lemon juice.

Use a toothpick to make dozens of holes in the top of a cake (see Moscow Nut Cake). Brush glaze over the top. Save remainder, which should be kept warm until serving time (it may be briefly reheated), when each piece of cake will receive an additional small offering. Brandy lemon glaze also makes a good topping for ice cream.

APIARY MUSTARD

Kendra is a Woolwich llama-raiser and beekeeper. She trains the llamas to go backpacking, and she makes beeswax candles and hand cream. She packages some of her honey in little bear-shaped containers and makes mustard out of the rest.

3/4 cup wine vinegar	1/2 t dried thyme
2 cups good Dijon mustard	1 T dried basil
1/4 to 1/2 cup honey	1 T dill weed or seed
2 or 3 cloves garlic	1/2 cup water
1 t salt	2 cups extra light olive oil

Combine everything except oil in a blender. Zap for 15 to 25 seconds, then slowly add the oil in a thin stream. (At this point, Kendra tastes and, she says, usually adds more mustard and sometimes more honey — and zaps again. She also prefers dill seed to dill weed.)

Pour into about eight 4-oz wide-mouth canning jars and refrigerate. TIE UP WITH STRING OR RIBBON, LABEL AND GIVE AS A GIFT FROM THE HEART.

PEANUT SAUCE

Use natural peanut butter that consists only of pulverized peanuts.

1/2 cup peanut butter at room temperature
1/2 cup hot water
4 T vinegar
Tamari soy sauce
2 T brown sugar or molasses

Mix peanut butter and water into a paste. Stir in vinegar, Tamari and brown sugar or molasses. Heat or use at room temperature as a sauce for steamed vegetables, grilled chicken or pasta.

The Owl And The Pussy-Cat
(Edward Lear)

The Owl and the Pussy-cat went to sea
In a beautiful pea-green boat:
They took some honey, and plenty of money
Wrapped up in a five-pound note.
The Owl looked up to the stars above,
And sang to a small guitar,

"O lovely Pussy, O Pussy, my love,
What a beautiful Pussy you are,
You are,
You are!
What a beautiful Pussy you are!"

Pussy said to the Owl, "You elegant fowl,
How charmingly sweet you sing!
Oh! let us be married; too long have we tarried:
But what shall we do for a ring?"
They sailed away, for a year and a day,
To the land where the bong-tree grows;
And there in a wood a Piggy-wig stood,
With a ring at the end of his nose,
His nose,
His nose,
With a ring at the end of his nose.

"Dear Pig, are you willing to sell for one shilling
Your ring?" Said the Piggy, I will."
So they took it away, and were married next day
By the Turkey who lives on the hill.
They dined on mince and slices of quince,
Which they ate with a runcible spoon;
And hand in hand, on the edge of the sand
They danced by the light of moon,
the moon,
the moon,
They danced by the light of the moon.

SWEETS

MRS. ROY ANTHONY'S ANGEL FOOD CAKE
BAKED FOR WINSTON CHURCHILL AT FULTON, MISSOURI

This is from *The Best in American Cooking* by Clementine Paddleford, a coffee table sized book that I checked out of the library 30 years ago. It was so endearing that I wanted to buy a copy. Alas, out of print. The only book available was a later, smaller edition that carried a different title and had the heart cut out — photographs that told the reader more than the recipes did.

The original edition profiled families that the writer encountered during a cross-country trip, which she probably took in the late 1940s.

12 egg whites
1/8 t salt
1 t cream of tartar
1 ½ cups sugar
1 cup sifted cake flour
1 t vanilla
1 t lemon extract

Beat egg whites with salt until foamy. Add cream of tartar, continue beating until stiff. Fold in sugar gradually, a bit at a time. Fold in flour the same way. Fold in vanilla. Fold in lemon extract.

Turn into ungreased 10-inch tube pan. Place in cold oven and turn to 325°. Bake one hour. Remove from oven, invert until cold.

QUESTION: Did Mrs. Anthony frost the cake?

ANSWER: I don't know, but Bobby says angel food cakes are open to interpretation. They may be iced, drizzled with a glaze, sprinkled with a little rose water, or sifted with confectioner's sugar. Garnishes of cosmos or daisy blossoms lend charm, and ice cream on the side is sweetly extravagant.

GOAT CHEESE CHEESECAKE

Anne, who lives in Orland, uses goat's milk cheese from her own Saanen goats and eggs from her own Plymouth Rock and Buff Orpington chickens.

The crust: 9 Zwieback (1 cup, crushed)
                1/2 cup sugar
                4 T (1/2 stick) butter, melted
                1 t cinnamon

Using a rolling pin, crush Zwieback between two sheets of wax paper or two kitchen towels. Turn into a bowl, stir in sugar and cinnamon. Stir in butter. Line a buttered cake pan (8 or 9 inches by 1 ½ inches — taller than average) with the crumb mixture and chill for at least an hour. (A graham cracker crust is also good. Use 1 cup crumbs.)

The filling: 1 lb goat cheese, softened
                3/4 cup sugar
                4 eggs, slightly beaten
                3 T fresh lemon juice

Turn cheese into a mixer bowl, add eggs and beat until thick and pale. Gradually add sugar. Add lemon juice. Pour mix into the chilled crust and bake in a preheated 325° oven 30 minutes or until center does not wobble. Let cool for 20 minutes while you turn the oven up to 400° and make the pièce de résistance, which is

The topping: 8 oz sour cream
                3 T sugar
                1 t vanilla

Blend ingredients and pour over cake. Bake at 400° for 8 minutes. Cool to room temperature, refrigerate.

MOSCOW NUT CAKE

More loaf than gooey confection, this cake, which tastes better the next day, goes well with tea — steeped in a samovar.

3 eggs	1/2 cup chopped walnuts
1 cup sugar	1 ½ cups unbleached white flour
1/2 t baking soda	1 t baking powder
2 t vanilla	Pinch salt
3/4 cup sour cream	1/2 cup fine dry bread crumbs

Beat eggs until thick and lemon colored. Gradually beat sugar into eggs. Stir baking soda and vanilla into sour cream. Add to egg/sugar mix, beating well. Stir in nuts. Mix flour, baking powder and salt, fold in. Fold in crumbs.

Turn batter into a greased 9 inch springform pan. Bake in a preheated 350° oven 35 to 40 minutes. (A 10 inch pan cooks a shorter-standing cake in about 30 minutes.)

Serve with Brandy Lemon Glaze, page 58.

A MISTAKE

One day in 1930 Ruth Wakefield started to make Butter Drop Do cookies at her newly opened Toll House Inn in Whitman, Massachusetts. On impulse she chopped up a chocolate candy bar and added it to the batter. She assumed the chocolate would melt. It didn't.

The chocolate chip cookie had just been created.

My son Pierre once turned out delicious cookies when he melted the butter before adding it. The idea was to turn frozen butter to room temperature in a hurry but, as Wakefield could have told him, it didn't work as expected.

Commit Wakefields.

LARGE CHOCOLATE CHIP COOKIES

1/2 lb (2 sticks) butter at room temperature
1 cup brown sugar
3/4 cup sugar
1/2 t salt
2 t vanilla
2 eggs, beaten

2 ¼ cups flour mixed with 1 t baking soda
2 cups (12 oz) chocolate morsels*
Handful raisins

Mix butter, sugars, salt, vanilla. Stir in eggs. Stir in flour mixture. Stir in chocolate morsels and raisins.

Scoop batter with an ice cream scoop and level off with a table knife or the edge of the bowl. (The latter method is speedy but takes practice to master.) Release into your palm, roll into a ball, flatten. Place on a greased baking sheet, making sure each cookie has room to expand. If you wish, bake just two or three cookies a day, leaving the batter, covered, in the refrigerator for up to a week.

Bake in a preheated 350° oven 10 to 15 minutes. DO NOT OVER-BAKE. Let cool 5 or 10 minutes on the sheet. Remove to a wire rack and continue to cool. Do not store until cookies are thoroughly cool or you will create cookie jar mush. Yield: about 16 cookies.

EGGLESS MAPLE HONEY COOKIES

1 cup (2 sticks) butter
1/3 cup maple syrup
1/3 cup honey
1 t vanilla
1/2 cup whole wheat flour
1/2 cup unbleached white flour
Large handful chopped walnuts
Smaller handful sweetened flaked coconut
2 ½ cups rolled oats

Cream together butter, maple syrup, honey, vanilla. Stir in remaining ingredients one at a time. Place rounded tablespoons of batter on a greased cookie sheet. Flatten each to about 1/2 inch with palm of your hand. Bake at 350° 15 minutes. Do not overcook.

Makes about 20 cookies.

* Mix in or substitute cut-up pieces of top-of-the-market semisweet chocolate bars.

TWENTY FOUR HOUR ICE BOX COOKIES

This recipe came down to Anne from her grandmother, who was born in Scotland and went to California as a bride. Anne and her husband moved from that state to Washington DC to Maine, where they raise the most charming, all white goats you could ever hope to meet. Anne's recipe for Goat Cheese Cheesecake is on page 63.

3 cups flour	1/2 cup butter at room temperature
1 t baking soda	2 cups brown sugar
1 t salt	2 eggs
1/2 cup shortening	1 cup chopped walnuts or pecans

Combine flour, baking soda and salt. In a large bowl cream shortening and butter together. Stir in brown sugar. One at a time, stir in eggs, beating well after each addition. Stir in flour mix. Stir in nuts. Line two small bread pans (about 7 ½ x 3 ½ inches) with wax paper, leaving overhang to grip on each side. Pack in dough, which is sandy and yummy. Smooth top. Refrigerate overnight.

Slice thinly and evenly and place on an ungreased baking sheet. You can pack any crumbles into the bottom of a small, ungreased baking pan or put them on the cookie sheet with the other slices and manually press them together into slices. (Ice box cookies have a good attitude and pop out of the oven formed into cookies no matter what.) Bake in a pre-heated 400° oven 8 to 10 minutes.

CONGO BARS

Bobby has substituted red, pink and white M & Ms for the chocolate chips and shipped them as Valentine's Day gifts to undergrad grandchildren. My daughter Joujou uses less sugar and chocolate and more nuts. Gretchen, a potter who lives in Brunswick, also feels that 12 oz of chocolate is too much; she uses only two-thirds of the package. I use the whole thing.

The recipe makes a *ton* of bars, as you can tell by the need for an 11 x 13 inch baking pan. Up to 45 or 50 if you slice them small.

1/2 cup + 2 T butter
1 lb brown sugar (16 oz box)
3 eggs
1 ½ cups flour
2 t baking powder
Pinch salt
One 12 oz package chocolate morsels
1/2 cup walnuts or pecans, chopped

Melt butter. Remove from heat and stir into sugar. Stir in eggs one at a time. Stir in dry ingredients. Add chocolate and nuts.

Turn into a well-greased 11 x 13 pan, bake in a preheated 350° oven 20 to 25 minutes. Cool, slice into squares.

LEMON SQUARES

The classic that pairs sweet with tart in perfect harmony. Do not add extraneous ingredients, if such recipes (they are out there) pass your eyes.

The crust: 1/2 cup (1 stick) butter
             1/4 cup confectioners sugar
             1 cup flour

Cream butter and sugar, stir in flour. Turn into a lightly buttered 8 inch baking pan, press down evenly all round, bake in a preheated 350° oven 15 minutes. Remove from oven, spread topping over the surface, return to oven for 20 - 25 minutes. Let cool before slicing into squares.

The topping: 1 cup sugar
             2 beaten eggs
             Pinch salt
             Zest of 1 lemon
             2 T flour mixed with 1/2 t baking powder
             3 T lemon juice

Beat sugar and eggs together and one by one add everything else.

SARAH BROWNIES

My daughter Sarah has been tossing raisins into brownies since childhood and now I do it too.

2 oz unsweetened chocolate	1 t vanilla
1/2 cup (1 stick) butter	5 T flour
2/3 to 1 cup sugar	Handful raisins
2 eggs, beaten	OPTION: Handful chopped walnuts

Melt chocolate and butter in a heavy pot over low heat. Gradually beat sugar into eggs. Stir in vanilla. Gradually beat this mix into the chocolate one. One spoonful at a time add flour and stir well. Toss in raisins. If using walnuts make certain they are tasty. Stale walnuts: ugh.

Turn into a greased 8 inch square pan, bake in a preheated 350° oven 20 to 25 minutes. Test with a toothpick or broom straw (if emerges clean, brownies bid adieu to oven). Cool. Cut into squares.

CAROB BROWNIES

Carob is a root product that many vegetarians use in place of chocolate. It comes in powder and bar form and looks just like the real thing. Carob lovers say it *is* the real thing. For the record, it contains no caffeine and has less fat and requires less sugar than chocolate. When used as below — eggless, with oil instead of butter and honey instead of sugar (a more processed product) — the result is a healthful snack that is welcomed by those who do not or cannot eat dairy (or caffeine). BUT IT DOES NOT FOOL THE CHOCOHOLIC.

2/3 cup carob powder
1 cup flour, mixed whole wheat and unbleached white
1/2 cup corn oil
1 t vanilla
2/3 cup honey
1/4 cup fruit juice
Handful chopped walnuts

Mix carob powder and flour, stir in oil. Stir in everything else. Bake in a greased 8 inch square pan in a preheated 350° oven 40 minutes. Cool, slice into squares.

A BRIEF COMMERCIAL FOR PIES

Pies have a cosmic shape that returns us to the beginning of time.

They present a crusty exterior that contrasts with a sweet, succulent interior. The fragrance as they bake fills rooms with nostalgia. Pies celebrate tradition — rhubarb pie in spring, apple pie on the Fourth of July, pumpkin pie at harvest, pecan pie on New Year's Eve.

Do not substitute margarine for butter or vegetable shortening in pie crust. Margarine is watery; pie pastry wants crisp.

Use creative thinking. Mix raspberries into peach pie, raisins into apple pie. Make a three berry pie.

My daughter Joujou once made a pie on impulse with roughly equal amounts of rhubarb, strawberries and bananas. The pie had no top crust, and she did not mix so much as mass each variety. An edible Gauguin. She later said she regretted the use of the bananas, which turned brown and slightly mushy. I thought they looked wonderful — and the taste was perfect. For the record, she made a whole wheat crust (recipe in her head) and used honey instead of sugar.

RHUBARB PIE

Rhubarb is so sour, 19th century Mainers ate it first thing in spring to kill their winter germs.

Pastry for a 2 crust 9 inch pie (page 119)
6 cups chopped rhubarb in 1 inch pieces
Half dozen or more fresh strawberries, chopped
2 T flour
1 heaping cup sugar
2 t cinnamon
Gratings of nutmeg

Line pie pan with half of pastry, trim edge to a one or two inch overlap.

Mix rhubarb with strawberries, flour, sugar, and spices. Mound into pie shell.

Make lattice strips with remaining pastry, lay over fruit, seal to edge. Trim and crimp. To catch overflow (rhubarb is the juicy pie's juicy pie) place pie pan inside another, larger pan. Bake in a preheated 400° oven 45 minutes.

PUMPKIN PIE

> *O, it sets my heart a'clickin' like the tickin' of a clock,*
> *When the frost is on the punkin and the fodder's in the shock.*
> James Whitcomb Riley

Pastry for a 1 crust 10 inch pie
2 beaten eggs
1 1/2 to 2 cups cooked pumpkin
2/3 cup sugar
1 t cinnamon
1/2 t ginger or nutmeg
1/2 t cloves
1 cup heavy cream
1/2 cup milk

Line pie pan with pastry but do not trim.

Mix eggs and pumpkin. One at a time stir in remaining ingredients. Turn into pastry shell, trim and crimp edges. Bake in a preheated 400° oven 45 to 55 minutes or until firm in center.

NOTE: See page 9 for directions on cooking a fresh pumpkin, which yields such thick, tasty pulp that you don't have to use eggs in the pie.

PECAN PIE

This recipe and the following one reveal how ingredients used in different quantities or ways produce the same product. I've also seen a pecan pie recipe that deletes corn syrup but calls for a cup each of brown sugar and maple syrup (plus 3 eggs, 2 cups pecans, and vanilla). I haven't tried it yet.

Pecan pie filling (like pumpkin pie filling, its partner in mischief) can be voluminous. Don't be rash and try to pile it all into one shell. Refrigerate excess and when inspiration strikes make pastry, roll out saucer sized pieces, give each a dollop of filling, pinch together over the top for an abstract appearance (these are not pies but freeform pastries) and bake 25 to 30 minutes.

Pastry for a 1 crust 9 inch pie
4 eggs
2 cups dark corn syrup (16 oz bottle)
2 T melted butter
1 t vanilla
1 ½ cups whole pecans

Beat eggs. Slowly add syrup, continuing to beat. Beat in butter and vanilla. Stir in pecans. Pour into pie shell. Trim and crimp edges. Bake in a preheated 400° oven 35 to 40 minutes or until firm.

CHOCOLATE PECAN PIE

Pastry for a 1 crust 9 inch pie
2 oz unsweetened chocolate
4 T (1/2 stick) butter
4 eggs
1 cup sugar
1 ¼ cups dark corn syrup
1 t vanilla
1 ½ to 2 cups coarsely chopped pecans

Line pie pan with pastry. Melt chocolate with butter in top of double boiler over hot, not boiling, water. Cool.

Beat eggs. Beat in sugar, corn syrup, vanilla, chocolate mixture and pecans, in that order. Turn into pie shell, trim and crimp edges. Place on a baking sheet, bake in a preheated 350° oven 45 to 50 minutes or until a knife comes out almost clean. The center should be slightly moist when the finished pie emerges from the oven.

COMMIT SIN: Serve with sweetened whipped cream on the side.

APPLE PIE

Pastry for a 2 crust 9 inch pie
7 or 8 tart apples
3/4 cup sugar
1 T cinnamon
Generous gratings of nutmeg
Eggwash (1 yolk whisked with 2 t water)*

Line pie pan with half of pastry, trimming edge to leave an overlap of one or two inches (doesn't have to be strictly even).

Pare, core and slice apples. Mix remaining ingredients and stir into apples. Turn into pie shell, mounding toward center.

Cut lattice strips (wider or thinner, to your choosing) with remaining pastry, lay over fruit in a woven pattern, seal to edge. Trim and crimp. Brush your latticework and crust with the wash in a willfully careless manner — you don't want to coat every inch. (Your pie would then look heavy, like a room with too much dark furniture.) The purpose of eggwash in your life is to provide burnt umber highlights on pie crusts. If you sprinkle the washed top with a few grains of sugar the pie then emerges from the oven with *sparkling* burnt umber.

Bake in a preheated 375° oven 45 minutes. Serve with the best vanilla ice cream you can find, or hard sauce (page 58).

* Eggwash has different versions; see Deep Dish Apple Pie.

DEEP DISH APPLE PIE

More or less 7 tart apples
1/4 cup sugar
1/4 cup brown sugar
1 T cinnamon
Gratings of nutmeg

2 T flour
Zest of 1 orange
1 T orange juice
2 T butter in bits

Pare, core and slice apples, mix with sugars, spices and flour. Place in a buttered baking dish that's about 8 inches square or round but deeper than a standard pie pan. Combine orange zest and juice, sprinkle over apples. Dot with butter. Place topping over surface but do not seal to edge of dish. For golden brown highlights, brush on a bit of eggwash composed of the remainder of the egg used in the topping mixed with 1 T milk or cream. Don't be shy with the brush; use swashbuckling slaps. Bake in a preheated 375° oven 45 minutes.

The topping: 3/4 cup flour mixed with 1/2 t baking powder into which you cut 1/4 cup (1/2 stick) butter and most, not all, of one beaten egg.

APPLE COBBLER

The works:
   5 cups peeled, sliced apples
   1/2 cup sugar
   2 T flour
   2 t cinnamon
   Grating of nutmeg
   1 T butter

The topping:
   1/2 cup flour
   4 T sugar
   1/2 t baking powder
   2 T butter
   1 egg, beaten

Stir together apple slices, sugar, flour and spices. Turn into a buttered 8 inch square baking pan. Dot with the 1 T butter. Mix dry topping ingredients, work in the 2 T butter with fingers, stir in the egg with a fork. Using a spoon, drop 9 portions of topping over the works. (It will spread during baking.) Bake in a preheated 375° oven 35 minutes or until crust is browned.

BASIC FRUIT COMPOTE

Apples	Berries
Pears	Melon
Oranges	Kiwis
Grapes	Bananas

Using several or all of the above (except for banana slices, which you should add just before serving to prevent their leaking and marring the cosmetics), pare and core as needed into squares and chunks. Grapes may be sliced in half lengthwise, melons cut in circular shapes with a melon scoop. Toss together in a mixing bowl, turn into a serving bowl.

It adds a lively touch to accent the rim of the compote with small fresh mint leaves or an arrangement of a few kiwi or star fruit slices.

To serve, spoon into individual glass dessert dishes. Pass a platter of small cookies or bars or a dish of chocolate mints.

FOR A SMALLER SERVING, use 1 large orange, 2 tart apples, about 1/4 cantaloupe and a half-dozen strawberries.

STRAWBERRIES WITH CHAMPAGNE

Sprinkle washed and hulled whole strawberries with a touch of sugar. Chill. Turn into a crystal serving bowl and drizzle on chilled Champagne.

RHUBARB ON THE SIMPLE

Gretchen serves this in stem dishes with cookies on the side.

Clean, trim 2 lbs rhubarb, cut into 1 inch pieces, cook in 1/2 cup water with zest of 1 lemon and 1 cup sugar for 6 or 7 minutes or till tender. Cool to room temperature, whir in a processor, spoon into individual dishes.

FRUIT DESSERTS

CHEESE AND FRUIT

On each dessert or salad plate — or a large platter — arrange the following:
Piece of cheese (gorgonzola, if you can get it)
Several slices of apple, pear, peach or mango
Handful of fresh berries
Spray of mint or several flower blossoms for garnish

PINEAPPLE FINGER FOOD

Peel, core and chop a fresh pineapple into bite size chunks. Arrange on a platter with a toothpick inserted into each one. (Use plain toothpicks; the dye in colored ones may leak onto the chunks.) Garnish with fresh flower blossoms and pass a small dish of chocolate covered espresso beans or chocolate kisses.

PINEAPPLE AND STRAWBERRIES

A famous love affair. Toss together pineapple chunks and strawberry slices and — an option — stir in a bit of sugar. Chill if not using immediately, serve in crystal stem dishes.

SIMMERED SPICED FRUIT

3/4 cup sugar
1 cup water
Grated zest of one lemon
1 stick cinnamon
6 whole cloves
6 whole allspice

OPTION: piece of vanilla bean
3 large apples
3 large pears
3 large oranges
Any number of grapes

Mix sugar, water and zest. Tie spices in a cheesecloth bag (or leave them free). Bring to a boil, add pared and sliced apples and pears, simmer

8 minutes. Do not overcook. The fruit should be tender, not mushy. Remove spices and vanilla bean, if using. Let fruit cool in its syrup.

Add peeled and sectioned oranges. Add grapes. Toss gently. Serve in a large bowl, garnished with fresh strawberry slices or mint leaves if such luxuries are in season.

Serves 12.

NO COOK FRUIT DIP

This came from the same source in Surry as the spanakopita recipe and is equally subtle. Said source, Jane, belongs to the ICFL Club - Ice Cream for Life, free. The membership was bestowed after she sent Ben & Jerry's a postcard suggesting they name an ice cream Cherry Garcia. After a three year development process the company marketed what turned out to be one of their best-selling flavors. Jane's favorite is Mango Lime Sorbet. Says she, "It's cool and dreamy and the perfect foil for Indian Food."

Because I like the way she writes a recipe, I left the following in her words.

3 oz cream cheese (low fat, Neufchatel or no fat work fine, although alter
taste and richness somewhat)
1 pint sour cream (ditto the above)
1/4 cup brown sugar (less is fine)
8 – 10 crumbled macaroons (Archway's are my favorite)
1/2 t cardamom
1/3 t cinnamon

Mush the things together. I often toss each item as listed into the food processor and allow them to piggyback onto each other. Let the finished product sit overnight (if you can wait that long) for best flavor. Serve cold or at room temp according to taste. Garnish with cinnamon sticks and mint leaves. Best fruits for dipping are sliced Granny Smith apples, sliced pears, chunked cantaloupe and honeydew melon, strawberries, grapes and anything else that appeals to you. This can be a whole lunch for three or four.

P.S.   Jane didn't sign her name to the fateful postcard, but the ice cream company found her by sending out word via notices in the underground Grateful Dead network.

PLAIN OLD DELICIOUS CUSTARD

The basic version of such elegant classics as crème renversée and crème brûlée. It looks tempting (it *is* tempting) served in old brown custard pots with a few berries scattered over the top. The pots, when you find them in junque shops, go for $6 and up.

4 egg yolks
2 T sugar
2 cups half and half, light cream or milk (or a mixture)
1 t vanilla
Gratings of nutmeg

Beat egg yolks with sugar. Heat cream to hot and s-l-o-w-l-y add to yolks. Stir in vanilla. Pour into four ovenproof custard cups and grate nutmeg over the top. Be generous.

Set cups in a baking pan and carefully pour boiling water halfway up sides of cups. Bake in a preheated 350° oven 45 minutes, or until surface is burnished with golden brown.

CRÈME BRÛLÉE

Unspeakably rich and a smashing spectacle as you crack the glazed surface and set the fragrance free.

3 cups heavy cream
6 egg yolks
6 T sugar
1 t vanilla
Light brown sugar (about 8 oz)

In top of a double boiler over hot water, heat cream. Do not boil.

Beat yolks and sugar together until very light and lemon colored. Slowly, carefully, stir hot cream into yolk mix. Stir in vanilla. Return mixture to top of double boiler and stir over boiling water until custard coats spoon, about 10 minutes.

Pour into a four or five cup shallow ovenproof dish. Cool to room temperature. Refrigerate several hours.

Cover with 1/4 inch layer of brown sugar. Set inside a larger pan, add ice cubes all round, slide under broiler till sugar caramelizes. This takes seconds. Watch. Do not let it burn.

Tap glossy surface with the back of a spoon to break. Spoon into serving dishes.

CRÈME RENVERSÉE

This creamy rich soft soothing smoothie of a molded custard is more awesome than any other desert with the exception of crème brûlée. Pile berries into the center of the mold and garnish the outside with delicate sprigs of thyme.

The caramel
    1/2 cup sugar
    3 T water

} Swirl together in a heavy skillet until sugar dissolves. Place over medium heat and cook, stirring occasionally, until mix turns brown. It is now caramel and scorching hot. Do not taste; you'll burn your tongue. Immediately pour into a 1-quart ring mold and rotate to coat.

The custard
    3 eggs
    2 egg yolks
    1/2 cup sugar

} Beat.

    2 cups milk
    1 cup heavy cream

} Heat to scalding but do not boil. Slowly stir into egg mix.

    1 t vanilla

Stir into above.

Strain into mold. Set mold in a pan of simmering water, bake in a preheated 350° oven 45 minutes or until a knife comes out clean. Cool to room temperature, refrigerate overnight. At serving time unmold onto platter: run a sharp knife around edge of mold, hold a damp platter over the top, flip. If crème lands off center, gently jiggle into place.

ZABAGLIONE WITH ROSE WATER AND RASPBERRIES

3 extra large egg yolks
5 T sugar
1/2 cup dry Marsala
2 cups heavy cream
Several drops of rose water
1 pint fresh raspberries
Fresh mint leaves

With a fork, whip egg yolks with 3 T of the sugar until lemon colored, about 5 minutes. Stir in Marsala. Place in a metal bowl over a pan of simmering water. Stir constantly with a wooden spoon until the mixture coats the back of it, about 5 minutes. Pour into a glass or ceramic bowl and stir occasionally until cool.

In a chilled metal bowl, whip chilled cream until it begins to hold a shape, then gradually add the remaining 2 T sugar and splashes of rose water. Beat until you can hold the bowl upside down and the cream won't slide out.

Gently fold the yolk mixture into the cream. When the operation is completed, spoon the zabaglione into 6 glass stem dishes. Spoon several raspberries over each surface (don't cover). Garnish each serving with a crisp mint leaf.

MOLDED CHOCOLATE SOUFFLÉ

Recipes that call for special equipment are a nuisance, but this soufflé, which requires a six cup bundt or other tube pan, does not annoy anyone.

Butter and sugar to coat	4 eggs, separated
4 oz semisweet chocolate	1/2 cup sugar
1/2 cup (1 stick) butter	1/2 t vanilla
1 T corn oil	Berry sauce (below)

Butter pan particularly well, sprinkle with sugar. Shake out excess.

Cut up butter and add with oil to chocolate in top of a double boiler. Cook, covered, over hot water until mixture has melted. Whisk now and then to blend.

Beat yolks in a large mixing bowl. *Gradually* — you do not want to fry the eggs — whisk in a bit of the hot mix. Whisk in a bit more. Slowly add the rest. Stir in sugar and vanilla.

In the bowl of an electric mixer, add a pinch of salt to the egg whites, beat until stiff, or until you can hold the bowl upside down and they don't budge. Fold a few large spoonfuls of egg white into the chocolate. Fold in a few more. Then a few more. ALWAYS FOLD GENTLY, LIFTING AND TURNING WITH LITTLE CAT FEET.

Turn into the prepared pan and bake in a preheated 300° oven 1 ¼ hours or longer, until the soufflé has risen and fallen.

Let settle in pan for 15 or 20 minutes, cover with a plate, flip onto a rinsed platter. Spoon berry sauce around base. Pour remainder of sauce into a small serving dish, pass around the table.

Berry sauce

Place thawed frozen raspberries or strawberries (use fresh ones in season) in blender jar or processor with a big spoonful of sugar and — option — a drizzle of brandy. Whir until smooth. If you like, add a splash of lemon juice or water for a thinner sauce. Refrigerate until serving time. Leftover sauce may be refrigerated or frozen for use with ice cream or waffles.

THE ONE AND ONLY APPLE PECAN LOAF

The preparation of this loaf calls for particular serenity and adherence to directions. It is worth the trouble.

6 cups peeled, cored, diced apples
1 cup chopped pecans
2 cups sugar

Mix. Let stand one hour. Do not omit this step and do not cheat on the one hour.

3 cups flour
3 t cinnamon
Several grates nutmeg
2 t baking powder

Mix, stir into above, combining well.

1 cup (2 sticks) butter, melted and cooled to lukewarm
2 t vanilla
2 beaten eggs

Mix and add to above, combining well.

Oil a LARGE (5 x 9 inch) loaf pan, line with wax paper, oil again. Turn batter into pan, bake in a preheated 325° oven 1 ½ hours. After one hour dust with a mix of 2 t sugar and 1/2 t cinnamon.

Let loaf cool in pan one hour. Do not cheat.

Remove from pan. Let cool one hour. Do not cheat.

Slice — it will be crumbly, intoxicating, fragrant — and consume as a dessert, as a complement to afternoon tea, or as your breakfast grain and fruit.

THE ONE AND ONLY APPLE CRUNCH

Don't even think of using another crunch recipe.

5, 6, 7 apples
3/4 cup rolled oats
3/4 cup brown sugar
1/2 cup flour
1/2 cup (1 stick) butter

Pare, core and slice apples into a buttered shallow baking dish. Mix dry ingredients. Work in butter with fingers. Pat over top of apples and bake in a preheated 350° oven 35 to 45 minutes.

You may substitute wild Maine BLUEBERRIES, or PEACHES, or mix up an APPLE/PEAR/CRANBERRY crunch, or whatever you wish. The cranberries do not have to be precooked but any crunch that contains them should bake for a full preheated 45 minutes.

A knockout when served with VANILLA ICE CREAM.

FOUR BAKED APPLES

Back when I worked for a small publisher in Princeton, NJ, I received a token Christmas present from a major publisher in New York. Hundreds of other editorial assistants received the same booklet, which featured holiday recipes "from various cookbooks." I was and remain pleased with the gift, and whenever I take it from the shelf I am drawn anew to the effortless recipes and simple black and white illustrations.

JUST BECAUSE IT IS A BAKED APPLE DOES NOT MEAN IT HAS TO BE A DESSERT.

Serve them right on the dinner plate with a congenial something like baked beans, or sausage and boiled potatoes with chopped parsley all over the place.

1/2 cup sugar + 1/2 cup water + 1 T butter
Generous sprinklings of cinnamon and nutmeg
4 large apples (Granny Smith is a good choice)

Gently boil sugar, water, butter and spices two minutes. Core and peel but leave apples whole (a melon cutter comes in handy here). Place in a small greased baking dish. Pour the hot syrup over apples, bake in a preheated 350° oven 45 minutes, basting twice.

RHUBARB BREAD PUDDING

This is an unusually tangy bread pudding, almost better than rhubarb pie.

1 ½ cups milk
2 eggs, beaten
3/4 cup honey
2 t cinnamon
Several grates nutmeg
1 ½ cups crumbs from whole wheat bread *
1 cup raisins
4 cups rhubarb cut into bite size pieces

Butter the top half of a double boiler. Mix all ingredients, pour into the greased pot, cover, cook over simmering water 45 minutes to one hour.

You can also bake the pudding, and you can vary the proportions of the ingredients. (See Apple Bread Pudding, below.)

APPLE BREAD PUDDING

Notice how the measurements differ from those in rhubarb bread pudding.

2 cups milk
3 eggs, beaten
1/3 cup sugar
Pinch salt
Big sprinkling of cinnamon (maybe 2, 3 t)
Big grates of nutmeg (less volume than cinnamon)
2 cups fresh bread crumbs
2 cups peeled, cored apple slices

Mix all ingredients, pour into a buttered baking dish, set inside a larger pan. Fill pan half-way up sides with boiling water. Place in a preheated 350° oven for one hour or until a knife tests clean.

You may include raisins or currents in the lineup of ingredients, and you may add or substitute berries. You may omit fruit altogether, for a basic bread pudding. If you do so, be sure to stir in a teaspoon of vanilla extract for flavoring.

* Remove crusts from bread that, in an ideal world, is four or five days old. Cut into cubes, tear into crumbs.

BREAD PUDDING WITH RASPBERRIES AND WHISKEY SAUCE

1/2 cup raisins
1/4 cup bourbon
8 cups torn bite size pieces French bread (1 or 2 baguettes — total of 1 lb)
5 cups milk
1 cinnamon stick
1 t vanilla
6 large eggs
1 cup sugar
Handful raspberries

Soak raisins in bourbon 30 minutes to overnight.

Put bread in a bowl. Drain raisins, reserving liquid to use in sauce. Add raisins to bread. In a pot mix milk, cinnamon stick and vanilla, cook over medium heat until hot but not boiling. Beat eggs with sugar in a large bowl. Gradually stir in hot milk. Discard cinnamon stick. Stir in bread. Stir in raspberries. Let mixture soak 15 minutes.

Turn into a 9 x 23-inch buttered baking pan, pat even. Set pan inside a larger pan, pour in boiling water to reach one inch up sides of baking pan. Bake in a preheated 350° oven 45 minutes or until a knife tests clean.

THE SAUCE

1 egg
1/2 cup sugar
1/2 cup (1 stick) butter, melted
1/4 cup reserved bourbon from raisin marinade.
(Add more bourbon if necessary.)

In a heatproof bowl set over simmering water, whisk egg with sugar until light and nearly doubled in volume. This should take about 3 minutes. Whisk in butter a bit at a time, then whisk in reserved bourbon. Remove from heat but keep warm over water.

Cut cooled pudding in 12 squares, transfer to dessert plates. Drizzle on warm sauce. (It may be reheated over simmering water in a double boiler.)

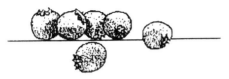

WILD MAINE
BLUEBERRY BUCKLE

Rosemary, who lives in Day's Ferry, Woolwich, usually doubles this recipe, baking it in a 9 X 13 inch pan (the basic recipe, below, calls for 9 X 9 inches). She says that using fresh plums in season gives equally ravishing results. Needless to say she uses only wild Maine blueberries. They're the tiny ones that spread over the ground among so many rocks and low-growing weeds that you can walk right over them and not know it. For further edification, See Robert McCloskey's children's picture book, *Blueberries for Sal.*

1 cup flour	1 cup wild blueberries (about)
1 cup sugar	1 cup heavy cream
1 t baking powder	Sugar
1/2 cup butter	Cinnamon
2 eggs, beaten	Juice of 1 lemon

OPTION: 1 peach, cut in small pieces and/or 1/2 cup fresh raspberries

OPTION: 1/2 cup fresh raspberries

Mix flour, sugar, baking powder. Cut in butter. Stir in eggs. Spread into a buttered 9 inch square pan. Dump blueberries-and other fruit, if using, on top. Sprinkle with 4 to 6 T sugar and 2 t cinnamon. Sprinkle lemon juice over that. Bake in a preheated 350° oven 45 minutes or until edges of buckle begin to look crisp and golden.

Cut into squares, serve while still warm with sweetened whipped cream on the side.

NOTE: Whip cream slowly at first (you don't want it to splash), then faster. When it begins to hold together, sprinkle on a dash of sugar. Continue to beat, add a bit more sugar (in all you should use about a teaspoon) and, if you like, a dash of rose water.

GRAINS AND

BEANS

AS

MAIN DISH

GRAINS GRAINS GRAINS

We eat grains directly in bread, crackers, cake, rice, pasta and cereals and eat them indirectly in meat: animals eat the grain and we eat the animals.

In ancient times, people spent hours beyond our belief sowing, tending and harvesting grain. This was in addition to hand milling, hauling water, gathering and carting fuel (wood, grasses, dried dung), hand crafting fireproof cook pots, and creating fire. No happiness kitchens for them.

Even as recently as colonial America, household members spent repetitious hours adding logs to and scraping ashes from beehive ovens until the brick walls glowed hot enough to bake beans, breads and pies for the next 12 hours.

In the history room of our local library I read about a 12-year-old Maine girl who cried herself to sleep from cold and hunger in January, 1731, while milling grain in a hollowed piece of tree trunk with a wooden tool. Her village had not yet built a central water powered mill. One existed 20 miles away, but the trail was obliterated with snow, ice, and fallen timbers, and passage was impossible.

Since beans and grains provide every nutrient we need to survive, it is no surprise that a lineup of combos evolved through the centuries: dal and chapatis in India, beans and tortillas in Mexico, hummus and pita in the Middle East, bean sprouts and noodles in China, baked beans and brown bread in New England, chili and cornbread in Tex-Mex, red beans and rice in New Orleans, and deep dish lentil curry pie on page 98.

BEANS BEANS BEANS

Beans belong to the leguminosae family that bears its seeds in pods. When we eat fresh green beans, both pod and seed go down the hatch. When we eat shell beans, we discard the pods and eat only the beans.

At the end of summer the plant dries up like an old stick, and the now rock-hard but life-giving beans must be revived by soaking.

Dried beans are known by a slew of aliases: legumes (French word for vegetables), dried peas, pea beans, and in England, pulses, from the Latin puls, for pottage - "pertaining to the pot." As for pease, it is an archaic spelling of peas and porridge is a variation on pottage.

> *Pease porridge hot,*
> *pease porridge cold,*
> *pease porridge in the pot*
> *nine days old,*

BOO ON BEANS

Some people don't eat beans because of a petty snobbism that took root in the upscale Victorian era: poor people eat beans.

As the 20th century gathered speed, animal protein began replacing vegetable protein. This happened for reasons other than snobbism: topography of the expanding west, growth of advertising, and because meat became safer, cheaper, easier to store. And people were sick of beans.

But America threw out the baby with the bath water when it lost its head over hamburgers and hotdogs. The more we became habituated to the taste of fatty flesh, the more we considered our forebears' diet a bore.

We are now the second most obese nation on earth (Russia is first) with death rates from heart disease to prove it. This cannot be pinned solely on the addiction to fat and flesh. Technology has stuck Homo sapiens in a sitting position.

Beans. They are not on drive through menus and they don't pop out of vending machines. And if you stress them by not soaking or cooking long enough, you can bet they will stress you.

HURRAH FOR BEANS

High in fiber, low in fat, profitable to you personally and the global village in general, beans are one of the simple things that hold the secret. On the day you begin to eat more pease porridge hot, you'll be helping children around the globe grow up with dignity and purpose.

THE LOGISTICS OF COOKING DRIED BEANS

SORT:
Rinse beans and be on the lookout for stones. You usually don't find any, but better you inspect than break a tooth.

SOAK:
With three exceptions (see chart, next page), beans should soak in water eight or more hours before they cook in order to break down the oligosaccharides that turn tumtums gassy. Cover beans generously with water to allow for swelling because they more than double in size as they soak. Before you put them on to cook, drain off the oligosaccharides-tainted water and pour on fresh.

QUICK SOAK:
There is a common method for obtaining the results, supposedly, of the all-night soak without doing it. I don't recommend and won't print it.

COOK:
Cover beans with water with an inch or more to spare. Bring to a boil, cover, simmer for allotted time (see chart). Add more boiling water if beans begin to look dry. At the end of the cooking period, drain excess (unless you are making soup, in which case you will have added a specific amount of liquid). Beans are now ready to join a casserole or salad.

GRAIN COOKING CHART

VARIETY	COOKING TIME	PROPORTION OF GRAIN TO WATER
Amaranth	25 minutes	1 to 3
Barley	20 to 30 minutes	1 to 3
Bulgur wheat	15 to 30 minutes	1 to 2
Cornmeal	10 to 15 minutes	1 to 4
Couscous	1 minute	1 to 1 ½
Cracked wheat	25 minutes	1 to 2
Kasha	5 to 10 minutes	1 to 3
Millet	20 to 30 minutes	1 to 3
Quinoa	15 minutes	1 to 2
Rice*	20 to 40 minutes	1 to 2 ½
Rolled oats	2 to 5 minutes	1 to 3
Wheat berries**	1 to 1/2 hours	1 to 3
Wild rice	1 hour or more	1 to 3

*   Natural long-or short-grain or basmati

**   4 cups wheat berries ground twice in a home mill equal about 6 cups whole-wheat flour.

BEAN COOKING CHART

Soak all beans overnight or for at least 8 hours unless otherwise noted.

VARIETY	COOKING TIME
Aduki beans	45 minutes to 1 hour
Black beans	1 to 1 ½ hours
Black-eyed peas*	45 minutes to 1 hour
Garbanzos (chick peas)	2 ½ to 3 hours
Kidney beans	1 to 1 ½ hours
Lentils*	45 minutes to 1 hour
Baby lima beans	1 hour
Lima beans	1 to 1 ½ hours
Pea beans (navy, great northern)	1 to ½ hours
Pinto beans	1 ½ to 2 hours
Soybeans**	3 to 3 ½ hours
Split peas*	45 minutes to 1 hour

*   Do not soak - not necessary.

**   Soak 24 hours. Between the long soak and the 3-hour-plus cooking period, soybeans try your patience. Even then they act ornery. Most vegans use fermented soy products such as tofu and miso, which are table ready in no time but provide the same nutritional wallop.

BANGOR BAKED BEANS

This is an American tradition that goes with cole slaw, potato salad, pickles, applesauce, brown bread, biscuits, cornbread, hotdogs, and apple pie — sometimes all at once.

The following formula is one honed from dozens of recipes that have camped in our house over the years. After experimenting with a variety of versions, and versions of versions, my conclusion was that it is hard to add molasses, brown sugar and bacon to beans and do anything wrong.

2 cups dried beans (Maine soldier, Jacob's cattle, or pea)
1 onion in chunks
Pepper to taste
4 T molasses
1/2 cup brown sugar
2 T mustard
1/2 lb bacon, chopped

SOAK BEANS OVERNIGHT. Drain, add fresh water to cover by a couple of inches. Bring to a boil, simmer 5 minutes.

Meanwhile, fry bacon. You do not want to cook it stiff, just relieve it of some of its fat.

Begin to ladle beans with their cooking water into a classic bean pot or other casserole. After you have transferred several ladles of beans and water, drain remaining water into a bowl and reserve. Turn remaining beans into bean pot and add just enough bean cooking water to cover. Set aside remaining water, which you may need yet.

One at a time stir other ingredients into pot. Cover tightly with a lid or double layer of foil. Bake in a 250° oven 5 or 6 hours. Check water level once or twice to make sure liquid bubbles at the surface. If beans start to look dry, add water from the reserve supply.

One hour before end of baking time, remove cover so beans brown on top. Or maybe they'll refuse to brown. Bangor baked beans have a mind of their own and turn out more, or sometimes less, liquidy. The "more" kind don't brown up as well as the "less" kind. Don't worry. One of the advantages of the recipe is that the taste is right no matter the appearance of the surface.

Serves 10, 12, 15.

MINERS' BEANS

This recipe honors Bisbee, Arizona, which has no lobster traps but whose brisk air suggests Maine.

Narrow streets pitch so steeply upwards that each house looms above its neighbor's roof. On one side of the street, 25 steps may lead from curbside to the front porch. On the other side, a railing keeps pedestrians from falling off. And a few miners' shacks perch precariously on boulders so high above street level that 60 steps may lead to the door. I think such houses were built by men whose work in the big copper mine was so imbued with desperation that they preserved their humanity by creating aeries in the sky.

In contrast to 19th century Mainers, who built homes from local forests, Bisbee's miners used materials available in the desert and their creative fantasies. The homes to this day are endearingly original.

2 cups pinto beans	2 T curry powder
6 cups water	1 T chili powder
1 lb bacon, each slice cut in half	2 bay leaves
1 lb sausage meat	10 shakes Tabasco
2 onions, chopped	1 t salt
1/2 cup Worcestershire	One 15 oz can chopped tomatoes
1/2 cup brown sugar	

Soak beans overnight. Drain, cover with 6 cups fresh water. Bring to a boil, cover, start to simmer.

While the beans simmer, mix bacon, sausage and onions. Stir-fry 20 to 30 minutes. (If you don't have an extra large skillet, do this job in batches.) Do not cook the bacon stiff. Drain fat, add the bacon mix to the simmering bean pot. Add Worcestershire, brown sugar, curry and chili powders, bay leaves, Tabasco and salt. Stir to blend. Bring pot back to a boil, cover, continue to simmer until the beans are cooked through, 1 ½ to 2 hours.

Fifteen minutes before the end of the cooking process, stir in tomatoes. Remove bay leaves. Serve with Buttery Cornbread, page 118.

BLACK SMOKY LIMA BEANS

Serve with applesauce and cornbread muffins.

1 ½ cups dried lima beans
6 to 8 slices bacon, chopped
1 onion, chopped
1/3 cup molasses
1/2 cup chili sauce
1 T mustard

Soak beans overnight in water to cover by several inches.

Drain, place in a pot with fresh salted water to cover. Bring to a boil, simmer, covered, 40 minutes (if beans should start to look dry, add more boiling water). Do not stint on the 40 minutes. Drain cooking liquid into a bowl and set aside. Turn beans into a bean pot or casserole. They will not be cooked through.

Sauté bacon and onion, drain fat, stir mixture into beans. Stir in 1 cup of bean cooking liquid, molasses, chili sauce and mustard. Bake, uncovered, in a preheated 350° oven 1 hour, or until black and smoky.

OSTENTATIOUS VEGGIE BURGER

Serve on a mustard smeared toasted sesame bun with a slice of tomato and shredded lettuce. Pass the mustard and pickles.

1 ½ cup lentils
5 minced mushrooms
1/2 minced green pepper
1 stalk celery, minced
1 carrot, minced
1 onion, minced
1 T each butter and olive oil
1 t salt
2 t paprika
1 t each cumin and coriander
3 T mustard
1/2 cup fresh whole grain bread crumbs
1/2 cup oats
1 egg, beaten
Several shakes Worcestershire

Simmer lentils in 4 cups fresh cold water 45 to 60 minutes, drain *well*. Let no steam remain to mess up the works. Sauté veggies in butter and olive oil. Off heat, stir in everything else. Chill to firm for an hour or more. Make patties. Sauté in a touch of olive or vegetable oil until hot and black-crisp, turning once.

HUMBLE VEGGIE BURGER

1 cup lentils
1 onion, minced
2 cloves garlic, chopped
1 t cumin
1 t chili powder
3 T mustard
Salt and pepper to taste
3/4 cup fresh whole grain bread crumbs
1 egg, beaten

Simmer lentils, onions, garlic and spices 45 to 60 minutes in 3 cups fresh cold water. Drain well, let all steam evaporate. Stir in mustard, salt and pepper, crumbs, and egg. Form 4 to 6 patties and sauté over high heat in the barest touch of olive oil in a skillet, turning once, till crisp, crunchy, and almost blackened.

EAT ON TOASTED BUNS with tomato slices, lettuce, mayo and mustard; on a bed of rice; on a slice of whole grain toast topped with catsup- and a pickle on the side.

You can refrigerate uncooked veggie mix for several days. Drain off any excess moisture before you make patties. YOU CAN ALSO FORM PATTIES AND FREEZE them on a flat surface — a cookie sheet does well; when each patty is frozen, wrap in foil. They may be defrosted one by one as needed.

SWEET AND SOUR BARLEY

This bean-grain combo goes down exceptionally well and with its canned beans and tomatoes is an effortless undertaking.

1 eggplant
2/3 cup barley
2 T olive oil
1 onion, or a bunch of scallions, chopped
One 15 oz can chopped or crushed tomatoes*
2 T dried herb of choice
1/4 cup lemon juice
3 T honey
One 15 oz can red kidney beans, drained
OPTION: chopped cilantro for garnish

Peel eggplant, cut into one-inch cubes, turn into a colander and toss with about 1 T salt. Let drain for 30 minutes, blot dry with a kitchen towel. If you omit this step, the eggplant's bitter juices may obliterate the allure of the sweet and sour taste.

While the salt is working on the eggplant, bring barley to a boil in salted water to cover, turn to a simmer and cook, covered, 20 to 30 minutes, or until it is softened and tasty. Drain, set aside.

Sauté onion in olive oil 3 minutes. Add eggplant, stir-fry for 3 more minutes. Pull off heat, stir in tomatoes, herb, lemon juice and honey. Return to heat, cover, simmer until eggplant is tender, 10 minutes. Stir in barley and beans, cook three minutes to warm and blend flavors. Add salt and pepper to taste.

GLOP AND GOO CASSEROLE FOR TWELVE

Nancy says people in Boothbay Harbor call this Aunt Martha's casserole. Do not put it together on the day you plan to serve it. The glop won't be intermingled with the goo.

16 oz noodles
3 lbs ground beef
About 30 oz tomato sauce
1 lb cottage cheese

16 oz cream cheese
1/2 cup sour cream or yogurt
3 bunches scallions, chopped
1/2 to 1 minced green pepper

Cook noodles according to package directions, drain, toss with a tablespoon or two of butter. Break up beef, sauté. Drain fat. Stir tomato

---

* The recipe serves four. To serve six, use two 15 oz or one 28 oz can.

sauce into beef and season to taste with salt and pepper. Mix together remaining ingredients.

Spread half of noodles in a buttered baking dish. Add cheese mix. Add the rest of the noodles. Add beef mix. Cool to room temperature, refrigerate.

On serving day remove casserole from fridge two hours prior to placing in a preheated 350° oven. Bake, uncovered, 45 minutes or until crisp and crunchy.

Perfect with green salad and a crusty loaf.

GLOP AND GOO CASSEROLE GONE VEGETARIAN

8 oz noodles
1 lb cottage cheese
1 lb sour cream
1/4 cup melted butter
One bunch scallions, chopped
Several shakes Worcestershire
Few dashes Tabasco
Grated Parmesan cheese
Fresh parsley or dill

Cook noodles, drain. Stir into everything else, which you have mixed together while the noodles cooked. Turn into a buttered baking dish, cover (lid or foil), bake in a preheated 350° oven 25 minutes. Uncover, continue to bake for 20 minutes or until the surface hints at golden brown.

Serve with a side dish of freshly grated Parmesan and another of chopped parsley or dill.

DEEP DISH LENTIL CURRY PIE FOR TEN

For this pie you should use a baking dish that pleases you — round, oval, square or rectangular; machinemade or handmade, dented utilitarian or oven-to-tabletop beauty. Just so the depth is greater than that of a normal pie pan and you are delighted with the whole affair.

BEGIN PREPARATIONS ONE DAY IN ADVANCE.

3 onions, chopped

3 cloves garlic, chopped

2 green peppers, coarsely chopped

3 T olive oil

4 ½ cups veggie or chicken broth

2 cups uncooked lentils

2 T chili powder

2 t cumin

2 t oregano

1 t paprika

} *

15 oz can chopped or crushed tomatoes

Pastry for a single crust 9 inch pie (page 119)

Chopped cilantro or parsley for garnish

Paprika for garnish

In a large pot sauté onion, garlic, green pepper in the oil. Stir in broth, lentils, spices. If you like, season with salt and pepper. Bring to a boil, simmer, covered, 30 to 45 minutes. Stir in tomatoes, with juice. Continue to simmer, uncovered, stirring once or twice, for 15 minutes or until mix has thickened. (If it looks thickened already, skip this step.) Turn off heat, check taste. More spices? Salt and pepper? Take action.

Cool to room temperature, refrigerate for a day to develop taste. Remove from fridge an hour or two before baking time, turn into an oiled baking dish. Make pastry, roll to fit your pie top. You may fit or not fit the edge of the pastry to the edge of the dish, but do cut steam vents.

Bake in a preheated 400° oven 30 to 45 minutes, until crust is rowned. Sprinkle with dropdead color combination of paprika and chopped fresh cilantro or parsley.

SUMMER CAMP MUESLI

The quantities here are downsized from the original line-up, which began with a few gallons of rolled oats (though no one measured) poured into a stainless steel bowl that was large enough for two persons standing opposite each other at a table to stick their arms into at the same time. The tossing was a storm at sea.

* This is the curry; for other curries, see page 161.

Eat with fresh fruit and plain yogurt at breakfast or any other time of day. Buy the dried fruits at a natural foods store for superior taste (no chemicals).

5 cups rolled oats
Raisins or currants
Chopped dried apples
Chopped dried apricots
Chopped dried figs
Chopped dates
Dried cherries
Dried, broken up banana chips
1/2 cup slivered almonds
1/2 cup flaked coconut
1/2 cup wheat germ

Use a selection or use everything but don't measure. Toss with your hands. Store in a transparent container with a tight-fitting lid and let it be a work of art.

NOTE: Commercial brands are over sweetened and cannot touch the above for a delicious taste.

FRIDAY STEW

2 cups pea beans
2 potatoes, chopped
2 carrots, chopped
1 large onion, chopped
2 cups chopped canned tomatoes, with liquid
1/3 cup olive oil
4 cloves garlic, chopped
Salt and pepper to taste
1 cup chopped fresh parsley

Soak beans overnight. Drain. Cover with fresh water, bring to a boil, simmer, covered, 1 hour. Add all other ingredients except parsley and simmer 20 to 30 minutes. Cool to room temperature. Refrigerate overnight or for the next two days. Reheat at serving time and pass a heaping bowl of chopped parsley.

NOTE: Friday Stew goes well with a round peasant loaf or hot biscuits. Or ladle it over couscous: Add 2 cups water to 1 cup couscous, bring to a boil, simmer, covered, 1 minute or until all water is absorbed.

ANGEL HAIR AND OLIVE PASTA

This superbly simple, excellent pasta dish comes from Peg's Italian cousin Matilda who, as a pharmacist in Schio, Italy, doesn't have time to spend long hours in the kitchen. Peg, a business woman in the health field, lives in the farming community of Benton. I met Peg at a Seattle ferry terminal — one of those, "You're from Maine? *I'm* from Maine" things that briefly touch the lives of travelers. Three days later we found ourselves at the same gate at the Seattle airport and talked all the way to Chicago, where we had tea at the airport and, for talking, almost missed the connection to Maine.

Chunk up two large ripe tomatoes. Cut up about a cup's worth of Goya brand green olives. Cook 1 lb angel hair pasta, drain, toss with the tomatoes and olives, olive oil to taste, and salt and pepper. Serve freshly grated Parmesan cheese on the side.

MISCELLANEOUS PASTA IDEAS

Toss hot pasta with pesto.

Toss warm, not streaming pasta with basic salad dressing (page 50). Add chopped or rolled anchovies, smoked fish, tuna, or cooked shellfish. Add minced scallions or red onions and other raw or crunchy-cooked vegetables. Sprinkle on a fresh minced herb for a dazzling finish.

Toss pasta, which you have cooked and drained, with butter, salt, pepper and freshly grated Parmesan to taste. In Italy this is called *Pasta, Burro E Parmigiano*.

FETTUCCINE ALFREDO

An old, proven, classic recipe.

To serve 2 or 3 persons, cook 1/2 lb fettuccine in boiling salted water 8 to 10 minutes — unless you use fresh fettuccine, which will cook up in 3 to 4. Drain, toss with 1 ½ T butter, salt and pepper to taste, and 1/2 cup warmed heavy cream. You may grate Parmesan to serve on the side.

STIRABOUT NOODLES FOR TWO

Cook 1/2 lb noodles of your choice, drain. Toss with 2 thinly sliced onions which you have sautéed in 2 T olive oil. Add 1/4 cup chopped fresh basil and salt and pepper to taste.

MUSTARD FETTUCCINE

Imperative that the butter be soft. Remove it from the fridge several hours before you start to operate.

1 cup (2 sticks) soft butter OR 1/2 cup each soft butter and olive oil
4 T mustard
3 cloves garlic, chopped
4 T minced parsley
5 scallions, chopped
2 to 3 cups broccoli florets*
Salt and pepper.
1 lb fettuccine

Combine butter or butter-oil mix with mustard, garlic, parsley and scallions.

Bring a pot of salted water to a boil, slowly add fettuccine. Cook uncovered at a full boil 10 minutes, or until the pasta is *al dente*. Add broccoli. After water has returned to a boil, cook one more minute. Drain, turn into a large skillet or into the same pot, cleaned and dried. Add the mustard sauce. Over low heat, toss until fettuccine is coated. Tastes even better when reheated the next day.

* Buy only fresh green broccoli. No matter how much you have planned on this or any other broccoli dish, if you arrive at the supermarket and the stuff looks tired, stay away from it.

SPANAKOPITA

When you make this Greek spinach pie, pronounced span-a-COPE-i-ta, it is as absorbing as being in kindergarten and producing a masterpiece out of goo and paper. Served hot, it is the glory that was Greece. Served cold the next day, or three or four days after that, it tastes even better.

The recipe, which feeds 15 to 20, comes from ICFL member Jane, who also gave me her No Cook Fruit Dip.

A good pastry brush is mandatory. So is pressing the spinach of all moisture. AND A FULL DAY BEFORE you begin to put together the spanakopita — a therapeutic procedure that takes about an hour — read the instructions on the package of phyllo for the defrosting procedure, which takes a day and cannot be hurried.

One 16 oz package phyllo dough, defrosted
1 cup (2 sticks) butter, melted

2 onions, minced
4 cloves garlic, chopped } Sauté.
3 T butter

1 t marjoram
1 t thyme
1 t oregano } Stir in.
1 t basil

5 eggs, beaten
1 cup plain yogurt
3/4 lb feta cheese, crumbled
1 lb cottage cheese } Mix, combine with the above.
Gratings of fresh nutmeg
2 packages frozen chopped spinach, drained
Salt and pepper to taste

START BY BRUSHING SOME MELTED BUTTER onto bottom and sides of a 9 x 13 baking pan. Place a phyllo leaf in pan (it will climb the sides), brush with butter. Repeat until you have stacked and buttered eight leaves. Spread on half the filling. Make another stack of eight, brushing with butter. Spread on remaining filling.

Fold down sloppy edges of leaves onto top of pie, or snip and discard. Snip away awkward bulk at corners. Add more layers of phyllo (all that's left) and butter, making sure you butter the top one.

Bake in a preheated 400° oven 25 to 30 minutes. Let rest 30 minutes to settle. Cut in rectangles.

INDECENTLY DELICIOUS PASTA

Liz is a former student of the dance at the Joffrey Ballet in Manhattan who now drives 20 miles from her Stetson farmhouse to a supermarket — and a dance studio. Her talent for and experience in choreography and design reveals itself in the films she now makes, the garden she tends (she is an ardent seed saver), and in this eclectically colored pasta dish.

1/2 lb angel hair or other pasta
5 T butter
2 carrots
1 bunch scallions - 2 if they're unusually small
6 large radishes - 8 if small
1/2 cup chopped, packed, very fresh dill
1 small, firm yellow squash
1/2 red pepper
Salt and pepper
One 15 oz can chopped tomatoes
2 T flour
2 cups light cream
2 big T mustard
Parmesan cheese for garnish

Bring a pot of salted water to boil, add pasta that you have broken in half, cook according to package directions (about 3 minutes for angel hair). Drain, toss with 2 T of the butter.

Meanwhile carve the veggies: carrots, scallions, radishes and squash in slices, red pepper in long strips.

Melt 1 T butter in a large pot and over low heat gently cook and stir the carrots, scallions and radishes for 5 minutes. Don't slave over a hot stove by stirring constantly, but stir every minute or two — the veggies must keep moving if they are to cook through. Stir in the dill, squash, red pepper, salt and pepper to taste. Cook and stir over low heat for a few more minutes. Stir in canned tomatoes, cover pot, cook for another minute. The vegetables want to be cooked but crunchy.

Meanwhile heat, do not boil, cream.

Make a roux with the flour and remaining 2 T butter, stir in hot cream — gradually at first, stirring until it is thickened into sauce. Off heat stir in mustard.

Gently combine pasta with the vegetable explosion (reds, white, orange, yellow, dashes of feathery green) and the creamy, binding sauce. If not serving right away, leave in the pot, reheat when ready.

Take a chunk of fresh Parmesan cheese out of the fridge, grate off enough to please your public, pass in a bowl.

CHOP SUEY HARD-WORKING MOTHER

I am tickled by the above name for what most people call "pasta and tomato sauce." But the woman who gave me the recipe is not most people. She is a resident Day's Ferry on the Kennebec, where she and her husband hand renovated a messed house (to start, the basement was flooded and frozen, with a bobbing washing machine, among other debris, held fast). Then they tackled a large shed in the yard. Had four kids. Then Laurie hung out a shingle on the shed and and began selling fine wines.

Her business represents the first retail one in the hamlet since the 19th century, when it featured a grocery store, post office, inn, ferry service, stage coach stop, smithy, one room schoolhouse, and church. To my mind, Laurie's shop, which also offers upscale pasta, olive oil, fruit drinks and so on, represents a first step in the renaissance of the neighborly economics American towns once took for granted.

The shop may offer fineries but Laurie cooks the easiest, fastest, most nutritious, least complicated meals for the family she can manage.

1 lb rigatoni or macaroni
1 lb ground beef
1 can condensed tomato soup
15 oz can stewed tomatoes*
15 oz can tomato sauce*

Cook pasta according to package directions. While it's on the fire, sauté hamburger till done and drain fat. Stir in the condensed soup, stewed tomatoes and sauce. Season to taste. Serve to growing children.

* Laurie says to use a smaller or larger amount if that's what you have in the cupboard.

RECUERDO
(Edna St. Vincent Millay)

We were very tired, we were very merry -
We had gone back and forth all night on the ferry.
It was bare and bright, and smelled like a stable -
But we looked into a fire, we leaned across a table,
We lay on the hill-top underneath the moon;
And the whistles kept blowing, and the dawn came soon.

We were very tired, we were very merry -
We had gone back and forth all night on the ferry;
And you ate an apple, and I ate a pear,
From a dozen of each we had bought somewhere;
And the sky went wan, and the wind came cold,
And the sun rose dripping, a bucket of gold.

We were very tired, we were very merry,
We had gone back and forth all night on the ferry.
We hailed, "Good morrow, mother!" to a shawl-covered head,
And bought a morning paper, which neither of us read;

And she wept, "God bless you!" for the apples and the pears,
And we gave her all the money but our subway fares.

GRAINS

AS BREADS,

PIE CRUSTS,

ET CETERA

HOW TWO PERSONS GO
ABOUT BAKING BREAD

When I met Melissa, she was raising a family, tending a cheerfully weedy garden, and teaching the art of bread baking at a place called The Night Kitchen. I was a newspaper writer assigned to interview a half-dozen home bread bakers.

"To bake good bread," said Melissa, "you have to be relaxed, be delighted with yourself. You have to choose a day when bread baking seems recreational, not perfunctory, when your schedule is open."

I never forgot the advice, or her habit of calling for "liquid," not water or milk. "Bread is composed of three things — flour, yeast, and liquid," said she. "Even if it's like lava, it's liquid." Melissa's doughs drank such liquids as vegetable cooking water, stock, applesauce and stewed fruit.

Another standout was Anne, mother of five who raised horses. She baked bread to provide an alternative after school snack to commercial junk, her principle being that one slice of homemade whole grain bread spread with honey was all the snack anyone needed.

"One of the assets of baking bread", said Anne, "is that you can be gone for three hours and come back and just punch the dough down again." She sometimes refrigerated dough to stop it from rising.

PAY A VISIT TO THE PUBLIC LIBRARY, check out a bread baking book, go home and study. Like learning to paint with watercolors, baking with yeast is elementary and only takes practice to bring pleasurable results.

KEEP TOSSING IN FLOUR as you knead — even if you have surpassed the quantity indicated (it is *never* enough). Knead for the full 10 minutes to heat up the dough, get it moving. Maggie, whose kids make bread in fanciful shapes — a snake going around a corner, for example — says that before her dough starts to rise she likes it to "really snap back."

BASIC BREAD

2 cups lukewarm water + 2T yeast
3 T butter at room temperature
1 T honey
Pinch salt
4 cups whole wheat flour
2 to 1 ½ cups unbleached white flour
OPTION: Handful of cornmeal

ALSO AN OPTION: Instead of 4 cups whole wheat and 2 or more of white flour, do the reverse, or use 3 of each.

Add yeast to water in a large warm bowl. Let stand 5 to 10 minutes, until it begins to bubble. Stir in butter, honey and salt. Add 2 cups flour, blend in with a mixing spoon. Add 2 more and blend that in. And so on. When dough becomes dense enough to work with hands, turn out onto a floured surface and knead, tossing in flour (either kind, and a little cornmeal if you wish) as necessary to keep dough from sticking to counter and your fingers. Kneading requires 10 minutes; work hard and straight through for best results.

Place in a greased bowl and turn once to coat all sides. Cover with a dish towel, let rise in a warm, never hot, place until doubled, 1 hour or longer.

Punch down, knead a few turns, divide into two parts. Roll into balls and shape into loaves, seam running along the bottom. Place in buttered loaf pans, cover with towel, let rise in a warm place 45 minutes to one hour until dough has risen above the tops of the pans. Fling on dashes of flour.

Bake in a preheated 350° oven 45 to 50 minutes. Loaf is done when it falls easily from the pan and sounds hollow when tapped. Tip out onto a rack (upside down dish rack works well) on its side. Do not eat while it is hot — bad for the tummy — though the temptation to do so may overwhelm your resistance.

POTATO BREAD

2 medium potatoes + 2 cups water

1 t salt

2 T butter

2 T honey

2 T yeast

4 cups unbleached white flour

2 or 3 cups whole wheat or soy flour, or a mix of both

Chop potatoes but do not peel. Simmer until tender, 10 to 15 minutes. Strain cooking water into a large warm bowl.

Peel and mash potatoes, stir into water in bowl. Stir in salt, butter and honey. When water has cooled to lukewarm, add yeast. Let stand 10 minutes before you begin stirring in the flours (see instructions for Basic Bread, previous page). Press out any potato lumps that rise to the surface. Stir with a mixing spoon and then on a floured surface with floured hands. Knead for a full 10 minutes, adding tosses of flour (any kind) as necessary.

Turn into a greased bowl, turning once to coat all surfaces. Cover with a dry towel (you can dust the underside with flour so it doesn't stick to the rising dough), let rise in a warm, not hot, place until doubled, 1 to 1 ½ hours.

Punch down, knead a few times, divide in half. Roll into balls, pat with dustings of flour, form into two loaves, place in buttered loaf pans. Cover with a towel, let rise about 1 hour.

Bake in a preheated 350° oven 40 to 45 minutes.

PUGLIA

This goes by many names, one of which, in New Jersey, is called Hoboken Bread. It would be false to call my loaf Hoboken because it's not so tall and crusty and lacks the trick — how do bakers (in Hoboken) give it that exotic appearance? Top crust peeled back like opened double doors to a second crust. A blazing hot commercial oven is part of the answer; technique is another. In the meantime, this loaf goes a long way toward making the home baker blissful at her chore.

(The neophyte should start with less complicated breads and try puglia after becoming familiar with knead and rise maneuvers.)

1 T yeast
2 ¾ cups warm water
1 T salt
5 ½ to 6 cups flour
Cornmeal

Sprinkle yeast over warm water in a warmed bowl. After it begins to bubble up (several minutes) stir in salt and, 2 cups at a time, flour.

Turn out dough onto a floured surface and with floured hands begin to knead. This is a sticky dough that does not firm up like most others. And you don't want it to become firm. But you must continue to sprinkle flour (the firm-up agent) onto the surface and onto your hands if the dough is not to stick like glue. Put this conflict out of your mind as you knead for 8 minutes.

Turn dough into an oiled bowl, turning once. Cover with a dish towel and let rise 1 ½ to 2 hours.

Punch down, knead gently a few turns, divide in two. Knead for a second. Plump, pat, arrange each ball on a cornmeal strewn cookie sheet. This time it will need to rise for about an hour. *If you think the dough hasn't risen sufficiently high, and it doesn't appear to be rising further, punch down and let rise a third time.* A half hour before you plan to slip the loaves into the oven, preheat to 450°. The oven must be REALLY HOT.

Slide the loaves into the oven, bake at 450° for 15 minutes. Turn oven to 375° and continue to bake for 20 minutes or until bread is crusty.

After 15 minutes in the oven most breads fill the house with the timeless smell of baking bread. This bread WILL SMELL LIKE IT'S BURNING after 5 minutes.

Good sliced, or sliced and toasted, or cut into wedges to accompany soup, stew, or soupy grain/bean dishes that beg you to dip into them with crusty something.

FRENCH TOAST

This serves three or four people.

4 eggs
1 cup half and half
1 T sugar
Several grates nutmeg
10 slices bread, more or less
Corn oil and butter

Beat eggs, stir in half and half and sugar. Grate nutmeg to your heart's content. Pour into a shallow dish. Remove crusts from bread and, one at a time, dip gently into batter to soak both sides. Fry in a mix of corn oil and butter, starting with 1 t each and adding more as necessary. Fry each piece of bread until it is gorgeously crunchy and hot, turning once. As each batch is done, remove to a warm place.

Serve with maple syrup and fresh berries, chopped apple or sliced bananas.

NOTE: If you slice the bread in half diagonally as it cooks (use edge of spatula), you can maneuver more pieces into the skillet.

P.S. If you serve bacon with the meal, cook it simultaneously and substitute freshly rendered bacon fat for the corn oil.

PANCAKES

Pancakes were the first thing I learned to cook, at age 9, so it was startling to discover a dozen years ago that Morgan's Mills, a well-known Maine brand of pancake and johnnycake mixes, calls for fruit juice and water rather than milk. I tried it and the pancakes turned out infinitely lighter than any I had made in the past. (My daughter, who has five children, never uses anything but fruit juice in all her baked goods.)

For the record, Richard Morgan came to Maine in 1978 to attend the Maine Organic Farmers & Gardeners annual Common Ground Country Fair. The event hit such a chord that he bought a gristmill in East Union, where he has channeled the energy of water ever since.

1/2 cup fruit juice + 1/2 cup water
1 egg, beaten
3/4 cup flour
1 t sugar   } MIXED
1 t baking powder
1 T melted butter
Oil and butter for greasing skillet

Beat liquid and egg together, add dry ingredients. Stir in melted butter. Sizzle 1 t each corn oil (or bacon fat if serving bacon with the meal) and butter in a skillet. Pour in batter, tipping skillet so batter runs quickly and evenly off center of cake onto hot skillet. Fry 2 to 3 minutes (bubbles appear on surface), flip, fry a few seconds more.

Use remaining batter, adding drops of oil, bits of butter, regulating heat as necessary. Serve with pure maple syrup to two or three persons. In season, scatter wild Maine blueberries onto the batter as soon as you have poured it into the skillet. Flip and behold wild blueberry pancakes.

THE PERFECT SCONE
(breakfast, not tea)

The cake (also called pastry) flour provides a light, silky texture. Failure to use it will not result in a failed scone but an ordinary one.

3 cups cake flour
1 T baking powder
4 T sugar
Pinch salt
1 1/2 sticks (3/4 cup) butter
3/4 cup milk or half-and-half
2 egg yolks, beaten

OPTIONS: Lemon zest, toss of crushed rosemary, handful of
               currants or wild Maine blueberries

Mix dry ingredients. Rub in butter with your fingers until the mixture is nubby. Stir milk into yolks; stir into flour mix. Stir in any options that catch your fancy.

Using a large spoon, scoop up batter and with the assistance of your index finger turn each of 7 to 8 rough, fat clumps onto a greased baking sheet. Bake in a preheated 425° oven 15 minutes or until peaks are browned. Serve warm with jam.

WILD MAINE BLUEBERRY MUFFINS

2 cups flour
2 t baking powder
1/2 cup sugar
2 eggs, beaten
1/2 cup milk
1/2 cup butter, melted
3 cups wild Maine blueberries

Mix dry ingredients. Stir in eggs, milk, slightly cooled butter. Fold in berries. Grease muffin tins, pile batter high (3/4 full) in each cup. Bake in a preheated 425° oven 20 to 25 minutes or until a toothpick comes out clean. Makes 12 to 14 muffins, depending on the size of the muffin tins.

TWO POPPYSEED LOAVES

Lo, who lives on the banks of the Kennebec in a cape cod house that long ago was floated upstream to the present site, gave me this recipe. Though you may take it plain or accompanied by a scoop of ice cream as dessert, the sweet crunchy texture is best realized when slices are spread with soft-ened cream cheese and made into sandwiches. *Sweet* sandwiches, but sandwiches nonetheless. You cannot stop eating them.

6 eggs
2 cups sugar
1 ¼ cups corn oil
1 cup poppyseeds*
1/2 cup fruit juice and water mixed
2 cups flour
2 t baking powder
Pinch salt
1 cup chopped walnuts
2 t vanilla
2 t almond extract

116

Beat eggs, gradually stir in sugar and oil. Stir in seeds and juice. Mix flour with baking powder and salt, add. Add nuts and extracts. Turn into two greased and floured loaf pans. Bake in a preheated 350° oven one hour or until a toothpick tests clean.

* Poppyseeds bought by the pound at a natural foods store are a better bargain than those packaged in jars at a supermarket.

SHORT'NIN' BREAD

> *Three little children, lying in bed*
> *Two were sick and the other most dead!*
> *Sent for the doctor, the doctor said*
> *Feed those children short'nin' bread!*
>
> *Mammy's little baby loves short'nin', short'nin'*
> *Mammy's little baby loves short'nin' bread.*
> *Mammy's little baby loves short'nin', short'nin'*
> *Mammy's little baby loves short'nin' bread!*

My mother used to sing this ditty to me, and I sang it to my children, when we made short'nin' bread. When it came time to write a book I decided to credit the songwriter. Off to the public library and a few surprises.

It is a black folk song that children once sang as they danced and played in a circle. There is no known lyricist or composer and several published versions, some of which use colloquialisms such as, "Sent for de doctor, de doctor said." Varieties on the lyrics abound: "Two little babies layin' in bed/One playin' sick and the other playin' dead." Or, "All them darlins' sick in bed," and so on.

Short'nin' bread was the slave version of the shortbread that the Old World Scots brought to the American south.

2 cups flour
1/2 t salt
1/2 cup brown sugar
1 cup (2 sticks) butter

Mix flour, salt, sugar. Sing "Short'nin' Bread." Work in butter with fingers until dough is smooth enough to leave sides of bowl. Press evenly into an ungreased 9 x 9 inch pan. Prick all over with a fork. Bake in a pre-heated 350° oven 20 to 25 minutes until lightly browned. Cool, cut into squares.

BUTTERY CORNBREAD

This is so moist and buttery that people who say they don't like corn-bread change their minds.

1 cup (2 sticks) butter
3/4 cup sugar
4 eggs
15 oz can cream style corn
1/2 cup cheddar cheese, shredded
1 cup flour
1 cup yellow cornmeal ⎫
2 T baking powder ⎬ Mix together.
1 t salt ⎭

Cream butter and sugar. One at a time, stir in eggs, beating each egg briefly with a fork before you add it. Stir in remaining ingredients.

Turn into a well buttered 9 inch square or approximately 8 x 10 inch rectangular baking pan. Bake in a preheated 325° oven 1 hour or until a toothpick tests clean. (The larger the pan, the faster the bread cooks.)

GRANDMOTHER'S FAMOUS
CRANBERRY BREAD

In November, read *Cranberry Thanksgiving* by Wende and Harry Devlin to the children in your family. Then everyone make bread. The recipe is on the last page of the story, and by the time you turn to it you'll be raring to go.

CROUTONS

Using not-up-to-the-minute-fresh coarse crumb bread, cut as many slices as you deem worthy. Unless the crust has the consistency of cement, do not trim. Cut the slices into bite size cubes.

Using 1 to 6 T olive oil, depending on the amount of bread, or an olive oil/butter mix, slowly cook cubes with 2 or 3 minced garlic cloves (don't burn garlic — you won't if you keep the heat low) until crisp. Turn off heat and, if you feel like it, toss the croutons with a few fingerfuls of dried herbs. Drain on paper towels, let cool. Scatter over a salad or individual servings of soup.

Croutons may be kept, tightly sealed, in the refrigerator and re-crisped in a 300° oven for 5 or 10 minutes.

PIE PASTRY

SINGLE CRUST 8 OR 9 INCH PIE
1 cup flour
1/2 t salt
1/3 cup + 1 T vegetable shortening
2 ¼ T ice water

TWO CRUST 8 OR 9 INCH PIE
2 cups flour
1 t salt
3/4 cup vegetable shortening
5 T ice water

TWO CRUST 10 INCH PIE
3 cups flour
1 ½ t salt
1 cup + 2 T vegetable shortening
6 T ice water

OPTIONS: Use butter instead of shortening, or a combination of the two. Do not use margarine.

When you measure the flour, mix in a tablespoon or two of whole wheat flour or wheat germ.

Mix flour and salt. Work in shortening or butter with fingers until mixture is nubby. Sprinkle ice water over top, stir with a fork. With floured hands, form a ball, firm by kneading gently a few times.

On a floured surface, using a floured pin, roll pastry (half of it if you're making a two-crust pie) out from its center, flipping gently several times to prevent its sticking to the surface. Each time you turn it over, toss a sprinkling of flour underneath and smooth it over surface with your free hand.

Work deftly. Do not lean on the rolling pin. As a cooking teacher once said to me, "Don't kill the dough. It's your friend. Be nice to it."

If holes appear in the pastry, which will form less than a perfect circle, cut off pieces from the edge and patch them over the bare spots with a dusting of flour and a touch of the pin.

When diameter of pastry is an inch or so larger than that of the pie pan, invert it into the pan. Add pie filling. Roll and add top crust if using. Trim and crimp edges.

LEFTOVER PASTRY IS VALUABLE if rolled by children, sprinkled with sugar and cinnamon, dotted with butter, sealed into half-circles, vented with a fork, and baked in the oven for 20 minutes. Apple bits, raisins, applesauce make other good fillings for mini-pies.

CLASSIC BISCUITS

2 cups flour	4 T (1/2 stick) butter	1/2 t salt
1 T baking powder	3/4 cup milk	

Mix dry ingredients, rub in butter with fingers, stir in milk with a fork. Stir into a ball, turn out onto floured surface. Firm up with a few kneads, tossing on fingerfuls of flour to keep stickiness at bay, pat or roll out to a 1/2 inch thickness. Cut with a biscuit cutter, cookie cutter (STAR, HORSE, DOG BONE, other shapes), or the edge of a drinking glass. Place in an ungreased baking pan; you may either separate the pieces or squeeze them side by side. Bake in a preheated 450° 10 minutes, or until golden brown. Leftovers are tasty for breakfast if split and sautéed in olive oil.

A pleasing option is to stir fresh snipped chives into the dough — or a teaspoon to a tablespoon of dried thyme, tarragon or rosemary.

EIGHT

CHICKEN AND

ONE TURKEY

MUSTARD CHICKEN EXTRAVAGANZA FOR FOUR

4 whole skinless boneless chicken breasts (2 to 2 ½ lbs total)
Salt and pepper to taste
3 T butter
4 scallions, chopped
1/2 cup white wine
1 cup heavy cream
3 T mustard
4 T fresh herb of choice

Split chicken in half lengthwise, sprinkle with salt and pepper. Melt butter in a skillet, add chicken, sauté 7 to 8 minutes, or until browned. Turn, sauté on other side 7 minutes.

Pile chicken onto a plate and keep warm. Except for a teaspoonful or less, discard remaining fat in skillet. Sauté scallions in the fat for 1 or 2 minutes. Pull skillet from burner, add wine, return to heat, cook and stir until wine is warmed, about 2 minutes. Gradually stir in cream. Stir in mustard. Cook for several minutes to slightly reduce and concentrate the flavors. Return chicken to skillet, simmer in sauce, turning once, for 1 minute. Sprinkle with the fetching green herb.

COQ AU VIN

You don't see coq au vin on menus anymore. Very old, very French, it requires the sort of long and steady time that has gone with the wind. But it is food for the gods.

8 oz cubed salt pork with rind removed
6 T butter
6 T olive oil
24 small white onions, peeled*
4 chopped cloves garlic
24 mushrooms with tips of stems removed
6 lbs chicken pieces with skin removed
2 t dried thyme
2 T fresh, minced parsley

Fresh parsley for garnish
1 bay leaf
1/2 cup brandy
Approximately 3 cups red wine
2 t sugar

Brown salt pork in butter and oil in a large heavy skillet. Remove with a slotted spoon, set aside. Brown onions, garlic and mushrooms in the same fat. Remove with slotted spoon, set aside.

Shake chicken pieces a few at a time in a bag of flour — about 1/2 cup — mixed with salt and pepper. Shake off excess flour, sauté 10 minutes per side in same fat.

Remove chicken to a large ovenproof casserole. Add salt pork, onions, garlic, mushrooms, thyme, parsley and bay leaf. Heat 3 minutes on stove-top to warm contents, then cover and place in a preheated 350° oven for 30 minutes.

Remove chicken and vegetables with a slotted spoon. Skim surface of any excess oils. Turn heat to high, pour in brandy. Avert your face, ignite brandy. After five or six seconds, put out the flame by pouring the wine over it. (THIS GIVES YOU A FEELING OF VAST ACCOMPLISH-MENT, ESPECIALLY IF YOU POUR RIGHT FROM THE BOTTLE, MEASURING BY EYE.)

Stir in sugar. Bring to a boil, reduce liquid by half by cooking over a high flame, uncovered. As a grand finale, fish out the bay leaf.

Now put everything into a clean casserole. Refrigerate overnight to de-velop flavor. Cover, heat through. Sprinkle with minced parsley.

* Easy peeling: dip into boiling water 10 seconds, plunge into cold water.

LEMON GINGER CHICKEN
This casserole is piquant with the taste of lemon, ginger and cilantro, and it has too many ingredients. CARRY ON REGARDLESS.

1 cup basmati rice
4 cups leftover cooked chicken in bite size pieces
Salt and pepper to taste
One 14 oz can artichoke hearts, chopped and drained

One 6 ½ oz jar marinated artichoke hearts, chopped and not drained
1 cup fresh, sliced mushrooms
5 or 6 chopped scallions, or 1 chopped onion
1/2 cup firmly packed chopped cilantro
1 cup milk
1 cup light cream
4 T butter
4 T flour
Juice of 1 lemon
1 t grated ginger root
Fresh or dried bread crumbs
2-3 T butter
1/4 cup grated cheddar cheese

Bring rice and 2 cups salted water to a boil, simmer, covered, 20 minutes or until moisture has evaporated and rice is tender. (If using packaged rice, follow directions.)

Butter a shallow 9 x 12 baking pan, add chicken. Sprinkle with salt and pepper. Add coarsely chopped artichoke hearts along with the liquid from the marinated version.

Sauté mushrooms and scallions or onion in 2 t olive oil or butter. This is called *duxelles* (dukes ELL). Scatter over top of casserole. Sprinkle on the cilantro. Spoon cooked rice over the whole thing.

Sauce: Heat milk and cream together. Make a roux with butter and flour, stir in hot liquid. When you have stirred it into a thickened sauce, remove from heat and stir in lemon juice and ginger root.

Pour gently over the top of the casserole. Scatter crumbs on top. Dot with butter. Scatter with cheese.

Bake in a preheated 350° oven 45 minutes or until bubbling.

Serves 8-10.

CHICKEN CURRY SALAD

The best chicken salad anybody can eat (the chutney puts it over).

Leftover chicken in bite size pieces
Celery, sliced
Raisins
Mayonnaise mixed with curry powder
A toss of chutney, any large pieces chopped
Bed of lettuce

Use more chicken than celery and more celery than raisins. Mix about 1/2 cup mayo to 1 T curry powder.

Toss everything but lettuce, refrigerate for several hours. At serving time, arrange lettuce on a platter or individual salad plates and pile chicken curry salad into the center.

CHICKEN PARMESAN

Chicken parts (3 or 4 lbs)
1 cup fine dry bread crumbs
1/3 cup grated Parmesan cheese
Salt and pepper to taste
3/4 cup (1 ½ sticks) butter, melted
2 cloves garlic, chopped

Mix crumbs, Parmesan, salt and pepper. Stir garlic into butter. Dip chicken pieces first into butter, then into crumbs. Arrange in a shallow baking dish in one layer. Drizzle a little remaining butter on top, bake in a preheated 350° oven 45 minutes.

Any excess butter and crumb mixture may be used as a topping for baked tomatoes (page 10).

CHICKEN BARBECUE

Chicken parts (3 or 4 lbs)
1/4 cup (1/2 stick) butter
1/4 cup lemon juice
1/4 cup vinegar
1/4 cup catsup
1/4 cup Worcestershire

Mix sauce ingredients, bring to a boil, stirring. Pour over chicken and bake in a preheated 325° oven 1 hour, or grill outdoors, basting frequently with the sauce.

GARLIC CHICKEN

Nothing could be easier to prepare, and the aroma is lovely.

One 4 to 5 lb roasting chicken
1/3 cup dried herb(s) of choice
2 T olive oil
Salt and pepper to taste
1 large head garlic
1 cup white wine

Stuff cavity of bird with an herb, or herbs, of choice. Truss legs and wing tips to body with twine. Rub one tablespoon olive oil over bird; season with salt and pepper. Use remaining oil to grease a casserole with a tight-fitting lid. (Or use a double layer of foil as a lid.)

Separate head (bulb) of garlic into cloves. Place bird in pan and scatter whole cloves of garlic, UNPEELED, around it. Pour in wine and 3 T water. Cover.

Bake in a preheated 325° oven two hours, or until done.

Spoon juices over individual servings of chicken (and potatoes, if you cook them on the side). Employ chunks of peasant bread to sop up the very last evidence. As for the garlic cloves, each person squeezes his own to render the pulp.

THREE HERB CHICKEN

1/2 cup sliced scallions
1/4 packed cup fresh minced parsley
1/4 packed cup each of 2 fresh minced herbs of choice
6 boned skinless chicken breasts, halved
Salt and pepper
1 lemon, sliced thin
4 T Butter

Mix scallions, parsley and the other herbs. Flatten chicken breasts by pounding *gently* with a mallet between sheets of wax paper. Arrange in a buttered baking pan. Sprinkle with salt and pepper. Place scallion mix on top. Now add a slice of lemon to each piece of chicken. Dot butter bits on top of that.

Cover with foil, or a lid if you have one, and bake in a preheated 350° oven 30 minutes.

THE TURKEY PIE

This is the best dish in the world to make with leftover Thanksgiving turkey. Follow directions carefully as it is not a follow your own bliss recipe.

Pastry for a 1 crust pie
3 cups hot chicken broth
4 T butter
1 chopped onion
1/2 cup chopped celery

4 T flour
2 T curry powder
3 cups cooked bite size turkey
1 cup heavy cream

Prepare pastry, roll into a ball, wrap in wax paper, put in the fridge.

Heat broth. Sauté onion and celery in the butter. Mix flour and curry powder and stir in. As soon as it sizzles, stir in hot broth, cooking and stirring until it thickens slightly into a thin sauce. Off heat, stir in cream. Then stir in turkey. Turn into a buttered ovenproof dish.

Roll pastry, fit around the top of the pie. If you seal the edges, which is not necessary but a creative choice, be sure to cut air vents.

Bake in a preheated 350° oven 30 to 45 minutes. Let pie firm up for a few minutes before you use a serving spoon to break into a crisp crust that releases the fragrance of hot cream and curry.

SEAFOOD

TUNA NOODLE CASSEROLE

This is it: the dinner prepared by more Maine mothers, grandmothers, and great grandmothers than any other.

1 onion, chopped	4 T butter
1 cup chopped mushrooms	4 T flour
1 T olive oil	Salt and pepper to taste
6 oz noodles	Juice of one lemon
1 cup milk	One 6 oz can tuna fish
1 cup light cream	2 or 3 slices bread, buttered
A fresh herb of choice	

Sauté onion and mushrooms in oil. Cook noodles (about 5 minutes — see package directions) in boiling salted water.

Heat milk and cream together until hot but not boiling. Melt butter in a heavy pot, stir in flour to make a roux; add milk mixture and continue stirring (a whip is the best tool) until you have a thickened sauce, about two or three minutes. Off heat, stir in salt, pepper and lemon juice.

Stir onion-mushroom mix into the sauce. Stir in cooked, drained noodles. Drain and flake the tuna, stir in. Turn into an oiled or buttered shallow baking dish roughly 7 x 11 inches.

Cut or tear bread into bits (discard crusts if you like), scatter over surface of casserole. Add about 2 T worth of butter bits. Sprinkle with salt and pepper. Bake in a preheated 350° oven until hot and bubbling, 25 to 30 minutes.

Scatter with a freshly chopped herb, or position a small spray in a corner of the steaming, crunchy, golden dish.

NOTE: This casserole also takes well to cooked leftover chicken; use about a cup of chicken pieces cut into bite size.

TUNA WIGGLE

This is one of several recipes that call for canned tuna fish, which is one of the most simple, delicious prepared products anyone can buy. Fresh tuna has its role to play (fantastic grilled over charcoal), but for a staple to whisk off your pantry shelf at a moment's notice, canned tuna cannot be beat.

4 T flour
Salt and pepper to taste
1/2 cup mayonnaise
4 T milk
6 oz tuna, drained and flaked
4 egg whites, beaten stiff*
Handful sliced mushrooms
1 small onion, minced
3 T butter

Gently stir flour, salt, pepper, mayo in a bowl. Add milk, stirring just until smooth. Stir in tuna. Fold in egg whites.

Turn into a well buttered baking dish, bake in a preheated 350° oven 40 to 50 minutes.

Sauté mushrooms and onions in butter, serve as a topping. Tuna wiggle also takes well to humble old lowbrow dependable faithful catsup.

* Make custard (page 77) or Béarnaise sauce (page 53) with leftover yolks.

SOLE BONNE FEMME FOR THREE

How many recipes do you have that serve *three?* No matter. Like recipes everywhere, the declared human serving capacity cannot be taken literally. If it were, the cook would have to weigh each portion and force feed the eaters like geese.

6 to 8 mushrooms, sliced
Butter
1 lb flounder or sole fillets
1 small onion, thinly sliced
Juice of one lemon
1/2 cup white wine mixed with 1/2 cup water
3 T butter
3 T flour
1 cup heavy cream, heated
Parsley
Sauté mushrooms in 1 to 2 T butter, set aside.

Arrange fillets, slightly overlapping, in a buttered baking dish. Place onion rings over the top. Sprinkle with lemon juice. Season to taste with salt and pepper. Pour in wine mix. Cover with a sheet of foil, bring just to a simmer (not a boil) on top of stove, place in a preheated 350° oven for 10 minutes.

Drain off liquid into hot cream. Make a roux with the butter and flour, gradually stir in hot cream and continue stirring until sauce thickens. Scatter mushrooms over fish, spoon on sauce, sprinkle with chopped parsley.

If you like, you may run the dish under the broiler for an instant to glaze the creamy white sauce with a hint of golden brown.

BOILED MAINE LOBSTER

Once on the Five Islands wharf my brother-in-law's lobster shell put up such resistance that he went into the cook shack, borrowed a hammer, came out, positioned his lobster firmly on the floor of the pier. Whack! Whack! Next to his kneeling figure a guy in orange and hot pink oilskins hoisted watery cases of fish from a boat below. People ate at tables all around us, children darted like minnows, an old dog napped. No one paid brother-in-law the slightest attention.

Buy one, one and a half, or two pound lobsters. (The meat of larger ones is not so tender.) Bring a pot of water to a rolling boil, grab each live crustacean from behind its head, plunge it into the water. Cover; after water returns to a boil, simmer six minutes for the first pound, three minutes more for each additional pound. Remove lobsters from the pot, set aside for a few minutes or until cool enough to handle.

Melt butter, stir in lots of fresh lemon juice, serve on the side.

Ripe field fresh tomatoes, corn on the cob, salad, beer, bread, and wild Maine blueberry crisp: a selection of the above will round out the Maine lobster dinner, and you.

DROP DEAD SHRIMP SALAD

The chemistry is perfect here. Measure well. Do not improvise.

2 cans anchovy fillets (rolled or flat)
2 t dry mustard
Salt and pepper to taste
4 T vinegar
6 T olive oil
Two 4 oz jars marinated artichoke hearts
4 cups cooked rice (1 ¾ to 2 cups uncooked)
2 lbs shrimp, cooked and shelled
2 cups celery, chopped
2 bunches scallions, chopped
4 hard boiled eggs
3 tomatoes
Crisp lettuce leaves

Mix anchovy fillets (discard oil in cans), dry mustard, salt, pepper, vinegar, olive oil, and marinade from the jars of artichoke hearts. Toss with artichoke hearts, rice, shrimp, celery, and scallions. Refrigerate several hours.

At serving time, line a platter with lettuce. Pile salad in center and garnish sumptuously with wedges of egg and tomato.

Serve with bread and chilled white wine.

TUNA STUFFED POTATOES
FOR THREE

Tasty, filling, nutritious, simple to prepare.

3 large baking potatoes
6 oz can tuna, drained and flaked
Several chopped scallions or a small minced onion
4 or 5 T mayonnaise
1 or 2 T mustard
1 hard boiled egg, finely chopped
Salt and pepper to taste
Sprinkles of Parmesan cheese and paprika

Prick each potato once or twice with a knife to ward off a messy oven explosion, bake in a preheated 425° oven 50 minutes. Cut a slice off top of each. Scoop bottom shells and top slices.

Mash potatoes in a bowl with tuna, scallions, mayo, mustard, egg, salt and pepper. Heap gloriously back into shells. Sprinkle each with grated Parmesan and paprika. Return to a 375° oven for 20 minutes or until hot-crisp.

Discard top slices, or spoon on leftover stuffing and bake at 375° with the Mamma potato shells.

SWELTERING DAY SHRIMP PLATTER

Suffering from heat and humidity? Go work in the kitchen. The intensity of the labor takes the mind off the heat.

When you prepare Shrimp Platter, the slaving over a hot stove part is brief: boil shrimp one minute, eggs six. This can be dealt with in the cool of early morning. By dinnertime, when the newspaper sticks to the tabletop, transfers print if pressed, and the refrigerator sweats, and a passing thunderstorm makes everything, including your brain, feel worse, all you do is place chilled goods on a plate. You don't even shell the shrimp. It's each to his own.

EARLY IN THE DAY: Mix up Cocktail Sauce 1940 (page 58). Trim veggies as needed, refrigerate.

Cook as few or as many shrimp as you please in shells. Hard boil some eggs. (Shrimp must simmer until they turn pink, about 2 minutes; eggs simmer 6.) For easiest shelling, plunge eggs into cold water; count to three, pour it off and add fresh cold water. Pluck eggs out of water one at a time and shell. Let shrimp and eggs cool to room temperature before you refrigerate them.

At serving time: line a platter or individual plates with crisp Boston lettuce leaves. Top it with some or all of the following: shrimp in shells; celery, carrot, and zucchini sticks; egg and tomato wedges, black olives, scallions.

Get out the chilled sauce and use as a dip. (This is a finger, not a fork and knife dinner.) Place a loaf of peasant bread on the table, provide a bowl for shrimp shells, eat on the screened porch.

SEAFOOD EN PAPILLOTE FOR TWO

2 fillets of sole (about 1/2 lb)
2 t butter
Six mushrooms, sliced
I clove garlic, chopped, or 3 scallions, sliced
White wine
Sliced lemon
Parsley

Cut aluminum foil into four squares twice the size of the fillets and put two together for a double thickness. Spread with butter. Place a fillet on each, sprinkle with salt and pepper. Top with mushrooms, garlic or scallions and a drizzle of wine (about 1 t per fillet). Arrange 4 thin slices of lemon over the works. Sprinkle with chopped parsley (1/2 to 1 t dried or about 1 T each if garden fresh).

Crimp foil over fish. Let no juice escape. Put into a baking dish and bake in a preheated 425° oven 10 to 12 minutes.

Serve with boiled new potatoes tossed with butter or olive oil and an herb, a green salad, a round peasant loaf, and a glass of white wine.

NOTE: According to *Larousse Gastronomique*, "papillote" (pappy-OAT) has a range of meaning: paper frills on end-bones of lamb, small pieces of meat enclosed in sheets of oiled white paper, and sweets wrapped in gold or silver paper which conceal a piece of paper with a poem or motto.

NOTHING TO IT BAKED FLOUNDER

Place fillets in a greased baking dish. (To save pot scrubbing, place on greased foil that extends up the sides of a greased baking dish. Afterwards, trash the foil and wipe out the dish). Dot with butter and season to taste with salt and pepper. Place thin onion rings and lemon slices on top.

Bake in a preheated 350° oven 10 to 15 minutes depending on thickness of fillets. USE THE OLD COOK-FISH-AT-10-MINUTES-PER-INCH-AT-THICKEST-PART RULE FOR THIS OR ANY OTHER FISH THAT YOU BAKE, BROIL, FRY OR SIMMER. One pound of fillets makes two or three servings.

SWORDFISH IN OVEN

Swordfish steaks or fillets
Salt and pepper
Butter
White wine

Allow 1/4 to 1/2 lb per person. Place fish in a well-buttered baking dish. Season to taste and dot with butter. Pour about 1/4 cup wine per pound of swordfish around it. Bake in a preheated 350° oven at 10 minutes per inch.

SWORDFISH IN SKILLET

Buy a fillet or steak — one large or several smaller ones. Fry in a mix of butter and olive oil at 10 minutes per inch, turning once. Serve with lemon wedges, parsley and beer.

FRIED SCALLOPS FOR FOUR

1 lb scallops
3 T flour
2 T butter
2 T olive oil

Use whole small (bay) scallops or sliced larger (sea) scallops.

Pat scallops dry. Roll in flour, shake off excess. Sauté in a butter-oil mix. Bay scallops will be done in two minutes, sea scallops (if left whole) take longer. Sprinkle with chopped fresh parsley and serve with squirty wedges of lemon.

OPTION: Skip the flour step and sauté scallops in sizzling olive oil.
Drain on paper towels, serve with tartar sauce (page 55).

STEAMED MUSSELS IN WINE
(Moules à la Marinière)

One of life's luxuries.

Butter	White wine
Minced garlic	Minced parsley
Mussels	OPTION: Shrimp

The following amounts are approximate and do not require precise measuring. The joy of the honest labor in preparing *moules* (mool) comes from the scrubbing in running water, the drizzling of wine, and the fragrance of garlic on the simmer.

A GUIDE, NOT A PROCLAMATION						
Diners	Mussels	Butter for sauce	Minced garlic cloves	White wine	Butter to swirl	Minced parsley
2	12	1 T	2	1/4 cup	1 T	1/4 cup*
4	24	2 T	3	1/2 cup	2 T	1/2 cup*
6	36	3 T	4	3/4 cup	3 T	3/4 cup*

* Tightly packed

Scrub mussels under cold running water, cut off extraneous threads (the beard). If you are using shrimp, shell, devein, and simmer in salted water to cover 1 to 2 minutes, or until they turn pink. Set aside.

Sauté garlic in butter in a large heavy pot. Add mussels and wine. Bring to a boil, cover and simmer for 6 minutes or until all shells are open. If there are a lot of mussels, shake pan a few times. Discard all shells that do not open. There's usually a good proportion of them — but nothing to be done about it. Out they go.

Turn mussels into warm soup bowls. Sprinkle with shrimp. Quickly reduce the liquid in the pot over a high heat and swirl in bits of butter. This will take a minute or two. Pour over mussels, sprinkle with parsley.

Serve with a crisp green salad, wedges of lemon, and a baguette of French bread to sop up the juices.

POACHED SALMON

In Maine we say, "Salmon and peas on the 4th of July." Salmon is always available but peas are not. Most years, our garden peas have not soaked up enough sunshine to be ready by the 4th. Oh, there will be two or three pods, 10 green peas. We feast on salmon and peas anyway, with peas from the farmer's market. (Farmers use plastic cover tricks.)

Allow ½ lb salmon per person for generous servings. Cover a piece of salmon (cut from the midsection if possible) with water. Add salt. Bring to a boil, cover and simmer 8 minutes per pound (or, calculated alternatively, 10 minutes per inch). It helps to poach the fish in a steamer with a rack that can be lifted. Otherwise, remove salmon as carefully as possible to a platter. Let cool 15 minutes, peel away skin and discard.

Garnish with exquisitely thin slices of lemon and red onion and sprigs of fresh crunchy garden parsley.

Serve with Hollandaise sauce (page 54), boiled potatoes sprinkled with parsley, and, on the 4th of July, garden fresh peas.

Excellent served leftover with leftover Hollandaise or lemon-doctored mayonnaise.

LEMON CRAB CASSEROLE

4 T butter
2 T flour
1 cup hot light cream
1 T mustard
Juice of two lemons
Salt and pepper to taste
2 cups crab meat, picked over
4 or 5 scallions, sliced
Buttered soft bread crumbs*
1/4 cup or more coarsely-chopped fresh cilantro

Make the roux, stir in the hot cream until you have a thickened sauce. Remove from heat, stir in mustard, lemon juice, salt and pepper, crab meat and scallions.

Turn into a buttered casserole or baking pan, top with crumbs, bake in a preheated 350° oven 20 minutes.

Scatter cilantro over top — *cover* the casserole with it — and serve to your public.

* Cut crusts from bread of your choice: two, three or four slices. Spread lavishly with softened butter on one side, tear into rough, crumbly pieces.

SHERRY SHRIMP CRAB CASSEROLE

This version of Lemon Crab Casserole substitutes the sweet, soothing taste of sherry for the tart one of lemon juice and mustard. It also makes enough sauce for each person to spoon excess over potatoes, carrots, and biscuits.

1 lb shrimp, shelled and deveined
1 lb crab meat *
14 oz can artichoke hearts, drained and chopped
4 T (1/4 cup) butter
3 or 4 large portabella mushrooms, chopped
5 or 6 scallions, sliced
4 T (1/4 cup) flour
2 cups light cream, heated
Fresh cilantro or parsley, chopped
1/2 cup sherry
1/4 cup grated cheddar cheese
1/4 cup grated Parmesan cheese + butter

Dump shrimp into a pot of boiling water, return to a boil and cook, uncovered, 1 or 2 minutes or till pink. Drain, mix with crab meat and artichoke hearts. Melt butter, briefly sauté mushrooms and scallions. Lower heat, stir in hot cream and continue stirring until you have a slightly, not too thickened sauce. Off heat, stir in herb, sherry, salt and pepper to taste, and grated cheddar.

Turn into the prettiest casserole in the house and sprinkle with Parmesan. Dot with bits of butter, bake in a preheated 350° oven 30 to 45 minutes or till sweetly sizzling.

* You may substitute two 7 ½ oz cans crab meat. As with the fresh, check for cartilage and discard.

SEVEN BOWLS OF FISHES

With biscuits or peasant bread, this makes a meal and will even serve eight. It's tastier yet when reheated the following day.

2 T olive oil	1 cup white wine
2 cloves garlic, chopped	28 oz can chopped tomatoes
3 onions, chopped	Salt and pepper to taste
2 stalks celery, chopped	1 lb haddock, chopped bite size
1 carrot, chopped	12 +/- mussels, scrubbed
1 T dried basil	1 lb shrimp, shelled and deveined
1 T dried oregano	Fresh parsley

Sauté vegetables in oil in a large heavy pot. Remove from heat, stir in herbs, tomatoes, salt and pepper. Return to heat, bring to a boil, simmer, covered, 20 minutes.

(If you're not eating until later in the day, or the next day, cool to room temperature and refrigerate. Reheat to boiling point when ready.)

Stir in haddock and mussels and when heat returns to boiling, turn down, cover and simmer 5 or 6 minutes or until mussel shells open. DISCARD ALL MUSSELS THAT DO NOT OPEN. (There's always a few. Bury them a couple of inches underground and your plants will explode with vigor.)

Add shrimp, continue to simmer for two minutes or until just pink.

Ladle into soup bowls (over rice or couscous if you wish). Sprinkle each serving with abundant amounts of chopped parsley.

MEAT

EAT MEAT DO NOT EAT MEAT

For reasons of updated thinking (the planet is a village and the children around the corner are dying), many people now eat sparingly of meat.

The declining consumption of animal protein may represent evolution of the species — as if a primal intuition is guiding us quietly away from the fresh kill that once constituted the major nutrient. In the Cro-Magnon era, to hurl the stone, to kill and feed on the prey was imperative if the tribe were not to starve and freeze to death.

The 21st century may be the first one to turn away from killings. Survival of the species may now depend on it.

Evolution trickles past unnoticed. But:

Most ELDERLY PERSONS focus the main meal of the day on meat.

BOOMERS struggle against hearing echoes of childhood - "Eat your meat!" Though they try, and often succeed in acquiring new habits, monkey wrenches hamper efforts to become happy, after half a century, with new products, palates and plumbing.

So many 30 SOMETHINGS are vegetarians that most Mainers don't take anything with meat to a pot luck supper.

Vegetarians are so numerous among the CHILDREN and TEENAGE counselors at the summer camp where I used to work as a cook that the kitchen staff provides a separate main dish for them at every meal.

❧

Evolution does not march forward like an army. Evolution is a clown — but march it does. Sure there are elderly vegetarians who credit their health to their diet. They *are* healthy, and handsome, and engaged in the world — but so are millions of meat-eating seniors. And for every 30-year-old who abstains from animal protein, dozens of his peers consume it.

Here's to vegetarians. Your example encourages the rest of us to think about the meaning of life.

ENGLISH STEAK AND ONION PIE

1 cup chopped onions
2 T olive oil
1 lb steak in bite size pieces
1/4 cup flour ⎫
1/2 t paprika ⎪
1 t grated ginger root ⎬ Mix in a plastic or paper bag.
1/4 t ground allspice ⎪
Salt and pepper to taste ⎭
2 cups potatoes in bite size pieces
Fresh parsley

Sauté onions in oil in a heavy pot. Remove with a slotted spoon, set aside. Sauté beef, which you have shaken heartily in the bag of seasonings.

Sir in 2 1/2 cups water, bring to a boil, cover, simmer 15 minutes. Add potatoes, return to a boil, cover and simmer another 5 to 10 minutes or until potatoes are tender. Off heat, stir in onions. Turn mix into an oiled shallow baking pan (8 inches round or 9 x 13 rectangle is a good size). Cover with pastry made as follows:

Mix 1 cup four, pinch of salt. Cut in 1/3 cup butter. Stir in a beaten egg. Roll out. Fit over pie, crimp to edge of dish, cut 3 or 4 steam vents.

Bake in a preheated 450° oven 30 minutes. Sprinkle with minced parsley for a glorious presentation.

OCTOBER POT ROAST

Prepare one or two days in advance for top flavor.

5 lb pot roast
2 T corn oil
6 carrots, chunked
2 onions, chunked
1 cup celery, chunked
1 green pepper, chunked
6 ripe, juicy tomatoes, chopped (or a 28 oz can)
2 cloves garlic, chopped
Herbs to taste

Over a high heat sear roast on all sides in oil in a heavy pot. Off heat, place vegetables and herbs (dried or fresh — more if the latter) around it. Cover and cook till tomatoes start to bubble. Lower heat, simmer one to two hours (pot roasts accommodate the cook with their flexible cooking time character). Turn off heat but do not remove lid for another hour. After contents have cooled to room temperature, refrigerate until ready to reheat.

Serve with boiled potatoes at a dinner that celebrates the harvest of gardeners and farmers all over the world. Sprinkle parsley everywhere, on everything, with joy.

APPLE CIDER POT ROAST

Because it spends 24 hours in a marinade before you cook it, the pot roast must begin its work two days before you eat.

1 1/2 cups fresh cider
1 stick cinnamon
6 whole cloves
6 whole allspice
3 lb beef pot roast
Flour for dredging
2 T corn oil
6 potatoes
6 carrots
6 onions
Fresh parsley

Mix cider and spices in a pot, bring almost to a boil. Cool. Pour over roast, marinate in a bowl in fridge 24 hours, turning once or twice.

Remove meat from marinade, pat dry with paper towels, sprinkle lightly with flour. Brown all sides in hot oil in a great big pot.

Strain marinade, discard spices. Off heat, add marinade to roast. Add potatoes, carrots, and onions. Bring to a boil, cover, simmer one hour.

Sprinkle every serving with freshly chopped parsley and pass sliced French or Italian bread.

APPLE CIDER STEW

Gordon, a naval engineer who lives in Woolwich, maintains a small orchard and makes cider every fall. Using an old hand press and bottling the stuff in containers that many people save for him all year, he performs the operation out of doors, beside his barn. Then he walks across fields and up and down the road and gives away the product of his labors.

2 lbs beef stew
1/3 cup flour seasoned with salt, pepper, nutmeg and cinnamon
3 T corn oil
4 peeled and quartered onions
6 carrots in chunks
4 stalks celery in chunks
2 cups fresh cider
1 cup veggie broth (page 35)
Chopped leaves of the celery
2 bay leaves
2 T dried tarragon
2 T dried thyme

Shake beef, a handful at a time, in a bag with flour. Sauté each in some of the oil in a stew pot. As each batch browns, remove. In same oil, sauté onions till bronzed. Stir in carrots and celery, sauté another minute.

Off heat add beef, cider, broth, herbs. Bring to a boil, cover, simmer 1 hour. Turn off heat but do not remove cover. Cool. Refrigerate for a day. Reheat, remove bay leaves, serve with boiled potatoes tossed with minced parsley. Scatter more minced parsley onto each serving of stew. Peasant bread to mop with is *de rigueur*.

HANDSOME DOG CARBONNADES FLAMAND
(FLEMISH BEEF STEW)

Your public will go crazy. Prepare two days ahead, refrigerate, reheat.

2 to 3 lbs beef stew, bite size pieces
1 T olive oil
6 large onions, sliced
1 ½ cups veggie broth (page 35)
2 cups flat beer
3 cloves garlic, chopped

2 T sugar
1 T thyme
2 T flour
2 T vinegar
Parsley

Brown beef in oil in a pot a little at a time, adding more oil if necessary. As each batch browns, transfer to a heavy ovenproof stew pot. Sauté onions in same oil, add to stew pot.

Mix broth, beer, garlic, sugar and thyme; add to the pot. Mix flour with vinegar, stir into pot. Bring to a boil, cover, place in a preheated 350° oven for 1 ½ hours. Do not remove lid. Let cool to room temperature. Refrigerate.

Serve with honest boiled potatoes, a Boston lettuce salad dressed with olive oil and fresh lemon juice, a baguette, and extravagant sprinklings of minced parsley over both stew and potatoes.

BOEUF BOURGUIGNON

This is the boeuf (beef) on the menu at the Café Boeuf (patrons pronounce it "Burf") on Minnesota Public Radio's *Prairie Home Companion*. It is an elegant stew that once a year is worth the love and trouble of preparation. Refrigerate for a day to bring up the delicate mix of flavors.

2 lbs steak in 2 inch pieces	1/2 cup flour
1 ½ cups red wine	1/4 lb diced salt pork
1 onion, sliced	12 small white onions
1 T dried thyme	12 whole or sliced mushrooms
2 bay leaves	3 cloves garlic, chopped
Salt and pepper to taste	1 cup veggie broth (page 35)
1 T olive oil	Fresh parsley for garnish
1 T brandy	

Marinate meat in a mix of the wine, onion, seasonings, oil and brandy for at least six hours. Remove meat with a slotted spoon, save marinade. Shake meat in a bag with the flour.

Cover salt pork with water, boil five minutes, drain.
Peel onions (see Coq au Vin, page 122).

In a heavy ovenproof pot melt 1 T butter. Add salt pork and onions. Sauté several minutes, transfer to a bowl. In same pot sauté mushrooms. Add. A handful at a time, sauté meat (add more butter if necessary). Drain fat, leave meat in pot. Add garlic, marinade and broth. Bring to a boil, cover, bake in a preheated 350° oven 1 hour. Skim fat. Add salt pork, onions, and mushrooms. Bake 20 minutes more.

Serve with green salad, new potatoes in the skin, and a long thin baguette. Scatter fresh minced parsley on everything but the bread, which is for mopping. To smear a French baguette with butter is an act of dishonor.

BOEUF EN DAUBE

The combination of orange, garlic, bacon and thyme intoxicates — and banish all thoughts of serving this stew, which is pronounced boof (rhymes with hoof) en dobe, until it has refrigerated at least 24 hours.

1/2 to 1 lb diced bacon
5 or 6 onions, chopped
1 head garlic, chopped
2 to 3 lbs beef stew
Olive oil
Grated zest of 2 oranges
1 T thyme
Red wine
Fresh parsley, chopped

Sauté bacon in a large skillet; drain fat, pat bacon dry on paper towels. Sauté onion and garlic in about 2 T olive oil in the same pot. (You don't want to cook it through, only bronze and coat it.) Set aside; dump the bacon on top of it.

Slice beef into bite size pieces (packaged beef stew contains chunks as large as small roasts). A batch at a time, sauté in a touch of olive oil in a heavy stew pot. Use more drops of oil if needed and, as it browns, add each batch to the skillet mixture. If you keep the heat high, using a tea-spoonful or less of oil and sprinkling the meat with a little salt, it will brown in minutes. Don't worry about missed spots. Artistic abandon is everything.

Stir ingredients back into the pot, add orange zest and thyme. Pour in wine not quite to the surface, 1½ to 2 cups. (In the interest of financial discretion it may be wise to use one part water to three parts wine, measuring by eye.) Bring to a boil, cover, simmer 1 hour.

After the daube has come to room temperature, refrigerate 24 hours or more. Before you reheat, remove any congealed fat. (If you drain the bacon well and use olive oil sparingly, there won't be much.) Sprinkle minced parsley generously over each serving.

AS PETER RABBIT AND OLD PARSLEY THE STAG * knew, parsley is an incontestably wonderful nutrient. It also cheers the daube and the cook with the immediacy of bright, natural color. Add more minced parsley and liquid from the stew pot to boiled potatoes that you serve on the side. Put a baguette on the bare table and tear off pieces as needed.

Serves 8-10.

* See *Parsley*, a children's picture book by Ludwig Bemelmans.

❧

There was an old person of Blythe,
Who cut up his meat with a scythe;
When they said, "Well! I never!" he cried, Scythes for ever!"
That lively old person of Blythe.

❧

STEPHADO

I had never heard of Greek onion stew until my neighbor Bobby walked over with two portions. She is a 70 something who designs and hooks rugs and gives them all away as easily as she gave me the recipe for stephado. Says me: "I've never heard of putting prunes and cinnamon in stew. Where did you get that idea?" Says she: "Oh, you know, we lived in Greece for eight years. "

The liquid is plum red and tastes subtly of . . . plums. Cinnamon, too. You mop it up with chunks of bread — do not even think of serving stephado without a loaf of peasant bread.

Olive oil
2 lbs beef stew
2 lbs small white onions, peeled*
3 cloves garlic, chopped
2 or 3 tomatoes, chopped and peeled **
I cup pitted whole prunes

Red wine to cover (1 to 2 cups)
3 T vinegar
3 sticks cinnamon, each about 3 inches long
OPTION: 5 each whole cloves and allspice, tied in cheesecloth
2 bay leaves
1/2 cup tomato sauce

Cut beef into bite size pieces See Coq au Vin for peeling white onions (page 122). Sauté beef, onions and garlic in batches in 2 or 3 T olive oil in a skillet. As each batch browns, transfer to a stew pot. (If you have a paella pan or other capacious pot, you can forget the batch business and brown in one step.) Stir in everything else. Bring to a boil and simmer, covered, one hour. Do not remove lid. Let cool to room temperature. Refrigerate for at least a day. Remove whole spices and bay leaves before reheating.

* If you cannot find fresh white ones, use two jars (16 oz each) pickled cocktail onions, drained.

** Use either garden fresh tomatoes or canned or home frozen ones, with their liquid.

SKI CABIN LEG OF LAMB

Leg of lamb
Garlic
Olive oil
Potatoes
Flageolets*
Boston lettuce
Lemon juice

Puncture meat in three or four spots, slip in slivers of garlic from two cloves. Rub meat with salt, pepper, a cut clove of garlic, and olive oil. Place in a roasting pan, cook in a preheated 350° oven at 18 minutes per pound for rare, 20 for well done. You may do a small roast (3 to 4 lbs) in a preheated 450° oven for 15 minutes per pound. If your roast is larger (5 to 6 lbs), keep heat at 450° for 20 minutes before turning down to 350°. Use a meat thermometer to insure thorough roasting.

Serve with boiled potatoes, flageolets, and a salad of Boston dressed with olive oil and lemon juice.

OPTION: Pass a dish of crème de la crème (page 56).

NOTE: Use leftover leg of lamb in shepherd's pie (below) or Scotch broth (page 39).

· A small white bean imported from Belgium, usually found in jars or tins at specialty food shops. A classic accompaniment, if you can find them. In Maine I cannot.

GRILLED LAMB WITH MINT

6 lb leg of lamb, butterflied by butcher
1 cup chopped fresh garden mint
1/4 cup lemon juice
1/2 cup dry vermouth
1/2 cup olive oil
1 onion, chopped
Melted butter and lemon juice

Rub lamb with salt and pepper, place in a non-corroding dish, sprinkle with mint. Mix remaining ingredients, add. Cover, refrigerate 24 hours, turning occasionally. Grill over charcoal, basting with the marinade and turning occasionally, 20 to 30 minutes. Serve with hot melted butter mixed 50/50 with fresh lemon juice.

SHEPHERD'S PIE

IF YOU'RE NOT KEEN ON THE STRONG TASTE OF LEFTOVER LEG OF LAMB but you've got it leftover, shepherd's pie is, hands down, the answer. It's also a good dish to put together, freeze, and bake when the need arises. (You may also use leftover roast beef and say SCOTTISH PIE.)

4 T butter
2 onions, chopped
4 T flour
2 cups hot broth (chicken or veggie)
2 to 3 cups cooked lamb in bite size pieces
3 cloves garlic, chopped

1 to 2 T dried rosemary or mix of rosemary and mint
Mashed potatoes
Fresh parsley

Melt butter in a heavy pot, add onion, sauté 5 minutes. Stir in flour to make a roux, add broth and continue stirring until you have a thickened sauce.

Off heat stir in lamb, garlic and herbs. Season with salt and pepper. Turn into a buttered baking dish and top with a splendid layer of mashed potatoes whipped up with salt, pepper, butter and milk. Parsley is another famous addition, though not strictly necessary because you'll use it later (see below).

Bake, uncovered, in a preheated 350° oven 30 to 45 minutes or until the pie is heated through and bubbling seductively at the edges. (If you have refrigerated or frozen the pie, bring it to room temperature before you put it into the oven.)

Garnish with a major sprinkling of minced fresh parsley. Even if you have whipped some parsley into the mashed potatoes, add more to the top after the pie leaves the oven. You can hardly have too much parsley, in this or any other dish. See page 148, PETER RABBIT AND OLD PARSLEY THE STAG.

ONE MEAT LOAF

The nonsense song *One Meat Ball* was recorded along with *Rum and Coca Cola* by the Andrews Sisters in 1945; it was based on *The Lone Fish Ball*, composed in the 1850's. One Meat Loaf is no nonsense but real good stuff.

1 ½ lbs packaged meat loaf mix – beef, pork and veal*
2 eggs, beaten
1/2 cup dried bread crumbs or rolled oats (or even potato chips)
1 onion, minced
1 cup minced fresh parsley
4 T drained horseradish
2 + dried herbs of choice
Salt and pepper to taste

Mix everything with your hands to craft a smooth oval sculpture.
Bake in a preheated 350° oven 1 ½ hours. Serve with catsup or other
gooey sauce. Good eaten cold in a sandwich with mustard and strips of
lettuce and a pickle on the side.

* Or buy 1 lb ground beef and ½ lb ground pork

SHERRY STEAK (CHICKEN OR SHRIMP) STIR-FRY

1 lb round steak
2 cloves garlic, chopped
Similar amount grated ginger root
2 T tamari soy sauce   } The marinade.
1 T sherry
1/2 t sugar
2 T olive oil +
About 1 cup scallions cut on the diagonal into 1 inch lengths

Cut meat crosswise into thin strips, stir into tamari mix until all strips are
coated. Marinate one hour or more in the fridge.

Heat oil in a skillet. Over a high flame stir-fry beef mixture for two or
three minutes. Transfer to a serving platter, blot dry with paper towels.
Add a drop more oil to skillet, stir-fry scallions for 30 seconds. Scatter
over top of beef.

NOTE: This formula works equally well with boneless skinless chicken
           strips or peeled shrimp. Chicken strips, which are packaged
           on the large side, crisp up faster if you place them side by
           side in the skillet and do not stir but bronze on first one side
           then the other for about five minutes per side.

ROAST BEEF AND YORKSHIRE PUDDING
WITH THE OPTION OF GOLDEN POTATOES AND ONIONS

This is the Christmas dinner I have prepared for many years.

ROAST BEEF

Cook an eye round or sirloin roast at 18 minutes per pound in a preheated 350° oven. For a more crisp surface, start roast in a preheated

450° oven, lower to 350° after 20 minutes and continue to cook at 15 minutes per pound. This is for a rare-cooked roast. Use a meat thermometer.

PUDDING

1 cup flour
Good pinch salt
2 beaten eggs
1 cup milk

} Mix, let stand 30 minutes.

Pour 1/4 to 1/3 cup of the hot beef drippings into a 9 inch square pan after you take the roast from the oven. Pour in batter, bake in a pre-heated 425° oven 25 to 30 minutes, or until puffed and golden. Cut into squares, which deflate with a sigh. Serve immediately.

NOTE: Keep an eye on the beef as it roasts. If you think it may not render enough pan drippings for the pudding to cook in, add a bit of olive oil to the roasting pan.

CRISP POTATOES

If you use small potatoes, leave whole; if larger, cut into quarters or in half lengthwise. Simmer in water to cover till barely done (10 to 20 min-utes), drain. Place in hot drippings as soon as you have removed the meat from the oven and ladled off the fat for the Yorkshire pudding. (Alternatively, you may tuck potatoes around meat during the last 10 minutes of the roasting process.) You want to brown and crisp them. Turn once to brown more than one side. The operation takes 10 minutes at 350°. Or turn off the oven and let the hot fat brown the potatoes in the oven for 15 to 20 minutes.

GLAZED ONIONS

Simmer whole onions 20 minutes till barely done, drain, place with pota-toes in the hot pan drippings. Turn them two or three times.

LOGISTICS

Don't worry if all you have is one oven. The roast will do fine sitting on top of the stove for 30 or 60 minutes (you can crimp foil over it to retain more heat), and the veggies may be kept warm in a covered pot or dish. Yorkshire pudding is worth the wait.

ST. PATRICK'S DAY CORNED BEEF AND CABBAGE
AKA NEW ENGLAND BOILED CORNED BEEF DINNER

The vegetable count is entirely arbitrary.

4 lb brisket of corned beef	6 turnips or parsnips
Whole peppercorns	1 head cabbage
6 potatoes	6 beets
6 carrots	Parsley
6 onions	

Place corned beef in a large heavy pot, scarcely cover with water, add a handful of peppercorns. Bring to a boil, cover, simmer 1 ½ hours. Skim cloudy stuff that rises to surface at the beginning of the boil.

Add whole, pared potatoes, carrots, onions, turnips or parsnips. (You can add both if it doesn't crowd the poor pot.) Return to a boil, simmer 45 minutes or until veggies are tender when pierced by a a knife. During the last half hour, add cabbage, which you have cored and sliced into thin wedges.

Cook beets separately: cut off all but two inches of beet tops, cover with water, bring to a boil, simmer, covered, 45 minutes. Drain, cut off tops, slip off skins.

Carve corned beef in thin slices against the grain, serve with the colorful array of vegetables and peppercorns (softened from the cooking and possessed of a pleasantly hot twinge at each bite). Sprinkle generously with chopped parsley. Serve with mustard, horseradish, green salad and a round, coarse grained peasant loaf.

CORNED BEEF HASH (what you eat the next day)

Put equal amounts of leftover corned beef and cooked potatoes through a food grinder, or chop by hand. Add a chopped small cooked or un-cooked onion. (To make RED FLANNEL HASH, add a couple of chopped cooked beets.) Stir in a tablespoon or two each of milk and flour to bind mixture.

Fry in 1 or 2 T butter or olive oil in a heavy skillet, patting down evenly, until bottom is crusty. Flip, cook other side. Pass the catsup. You may also bake hash in a greased baking dish at 350° for 30 minutes or until top looks crusty.

NICE OLD TRADITION: Serve each portion topped with a poached egg. *Then* pass the catsup.

SUNDRY SOUFFLÉS,

CURRIES, CRISPS

AND

NON-EDIBLES

MID MORNING VEGGIE COCKTAIL

Drink hot in a mug on a cold day. Drink cold in a glass, garnished with a slice of lemon, on a hot day.

Though the recipe yields enough for eight to ten persons, you can brew up a single portion using a pinch of sugar and a splash of vinegar — perhaps a grind of pepper. (Forget the other ingredients.) As for Lo, whose kitchen looks out onto the Kennebec River, she makes it by the multiple gallons and serves it, with tea and munchies, at her annual Christmas coffee bash for women. Lo invites so many people, she has to give the party on two consecutive days.

2 qts tomato juice*
2 t sugar
1 T vinegar
1 onion, chunked
5 whole cloves
Piece cinnamon stick

Stir everything together in a large pot, bring to a boil, simmer, uncovered, 20 minutes or until slightly reduced and thickened. Stir several times during cooking process. Let cool slightly before straining into a pitcher (discard spices and onion). Tomato cocktail may be refrigerated and reheated.

*   It is worth the cost to buy the best brand. This information comes from Ruth in West Bath, who gave me the recipe.

DRINKS HOT AND COLD

FAITHFUL LEMONADE

Mix 1 cup fresh lemon juice (a half dozen or more lemons), 1 cup sugar, 2 quarts water and 1 thinly sliced lemon. Refrigerate for several hours and pour over ice in glasses. For ginger lemonade, peel a piece of ginger root, cut into 6 pieces, mix with 1/2 cup water, bring to a boil, remove from heat, let cool for 15 minutes. Remove ginger root pieces, add the liquid to the cold lemonade. For sparkling lemonade, use sparkling water instead of fresh.

SMOOTHIE

Soothing in the extreme on a hot day and a lunch onto itself, the smoothie is amenable to unmeasured amounts and the ingredients themselves are open to discussion. Some people use milk, others add vanilla extract or honey. This version, which to me is the best one, came from Maryanne, who is Swiss and pronounces it MARY Anne, and who lives in Warren. And leads hiking tours in the Alps.

3 to 4 T fruit juice
2/3 cup good unflavored yogurt
1 banana
1 or 2 peeled and chopped peaches, or several cut up strawberries, or a handful of raspberries.

Zap everything in a processor or blender for a few seconds, pour into a large drinking glass.

MULLED CIDER

For each serving, heat one mugful fresh apple cider, 3 whole allspice, 3 whole cloves and a piece of cinnamon stick. Heat almost to boiling, strain into a mug. The spices may be used a few more times before you discard them. If you make a lot of mulled cider, store allspice, cloves and cinnamon sticks together in a jar. Not only is this convenient but every time you open the jar, fragrance happens. The one thing to avoid is leaving the spices too long in the pot of cider (if you have leftover). They will over-spice the drink and it won't be so tasty.

HOT RED WINE

For each serving, heat — do not boil — 2/3 cup red wine, a lemon peel and 1/2 t sugar. Pour into warmed mugs.

SANDWICH FILLINGS

TUNA CREAM CHEESE

Process one 6 oz can tuna, 4 oz cream cheese, 1 T olive oil, 2 t fresh lemon juice, salt and pepper (or a touch of cayenne) to taste and, if you like, a handful of drained capers.

Or stir up the traditional tuna, chopped celery, chopped scallions (or touch of minced onion), chopped hard boiled egg and mayonnaise. A fine addition is chopped pickles or a bit of chutney and curry powder.

EGG SALAD

Mix 6 chopped hard boiled eggs with 2 stalks diced celery, 1 small minced onion (or 2 to 3 scallions), salt and pepper to taste and 1/3 to 1/2 cup mayonnaise which you have mixed with a tablespoon of mustard. In place of or in addition to mustard, add 1 T horseradish. Spread on pumpernickel bread, the darker the better. A slice of dill pickle on the side is imperative.

GUSSIED UP CREAM CHEESE

Mix any quantity you wish of room temperature cream cheese with chopped green olives, or chopped dried fruit and/or chopped nuts. Minced garlic makes a wonderful addition, as does butter. If you mix 3 parts cream cheese with 1 part butter, stir in minced garlic (use a press, if you have one, to reap the juices as well as the pulp) and dried herbs to taste, and let it season in the fridge for a day, you have a delicious dip.

GUSSIED UP PEANUT BUTTER

Mix in broken bits of dried banana chips and/or chopped dried apricots. Serve with finely cut strips of lettuce. Lettuce does wonders for peanut butter.

THREE RECIPES FOR CURRY POWDER

Mix everything together:

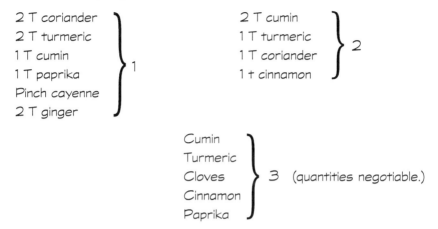

2 T coriander
2 T turmeric
1 T cumin
1 T paprika
Pinch cayenne
2 T ginger
} 1

2 T cumin
1 T turmeric
1 T coriander
1 t cinnamon
} 2

Cumin
Turmeric
Cloves
Cinnamon
Paprika
} 3 (quantities negotiable.)

Use ground, not whole spices, and strictly fresh ones. (TOSS OUT
ANY SPICES AND DRIED HERBS THAT ARE MORE THAN A
YEAR OLD. THEY HAVE LOST THEIR POWER.) Bear in mind that
the best way to measure is by eye. Mixing curry powder is a serendipitous ritual.

THREE HERB AND SPICE IDEAS

1) The best herb combination in the world to add to salads is comprised of
fairly equal amounts of fresh PARSLEY, CHIVES, TARRAGON AND
CHERVIL.

2) A pleasing standby (keep in a pint jar and use all winter) is a more or
less equal mix of dried

thyme
marjoram
parsley
oregano
sage
basil
rosemary

3) In a mortar and pestle grind equal amounts of coriander and cumin seeds
with a lesser amount of peppercorns. Good for rubbing into grilled meat.

QUICHE LORRAINE FOR REAL WOMEN

Quiche Lorraine is to other quiches what a Rolls Royce is to a bicycle. Do not eat big American apple pie pieces and do not eat as a main course. Don't serve potato chips on the side. Emulate the French: slice quiche into slender pieces and serve as an appetizer.

Pastry for a 1 crust 9 inch pie
6 chopped strips bacon
6 oz Gruyère (cut to order at a specialty store, if possible)
3 eggs, beaten
Several grates nutmeg
Salt and pepper to taste
1 ½ cups heavy cream

Line a flan ring with pastry. Sauté bacon, drain on paper towels. Place in bottom of pie shell. Scatter cheese, in pieces, on top of bacon. Beat nutmeg, salt and pepper into eggs. Pour through a strainer into shell. Or save time by not straining. If you wish, add a tablespoon of butter, in bits, to surface.

Bake in a preheated 375° oven 35 to 45 minutes or till quiche is puffed and a knife comes out clean. Let stand 30 minutes before cutting.

Marvelous served hot or cold.

COUNTRY PIZZA FOR REAL MEN

Even a 200 pound man must eat this slowly and wisely.

pastry for a 2 crust 9 inch pie
2 lbs ricotta cheese
3 eggs
1/2 lb sweet Italian sausage, cooked and chopped
1/2 lb lean pork meat, cooked and cubed
1/4 cup grated Parmesan cheese
1/4 lb diced prosciutto
1/2 lb cubed mozzarella cheese
Fresh parsley

Beat ricotta and eggs together until smooth and well blended. Add remaining ingredients except for parsley, which will be used as a garnish and to settle the stomach.

Line a square 9 x 9 x 2 inch pan with two-thirds of the pastry dough. Add pizza mix. Place remaining dough on top. Trim edges and cut air vents. Bake in a preheated 400° oven 20 minutes, turn heat to 325° and bake 40 to 50 minutes longer. Remove from oven and let cool at least 15 minutes before cutting into two inch squares. Serve each piece topped with a plump sprig of parsley.

Good eaten hot or cold.

SOUFFLÉ AU FROMAGE
(Cheese Soufflé)

Words cannot describe the drama of this dish, which from a diner's point of view is not only a piece of theater but unspeakably delicious.

From the cook's point of view it's a tough cookie. Timing must be exact, and it's impossible to work on any part of it in advance. The cook must conjure precisely how long the prep work will take (including the cooling) and exactly when everyone will sit down to eat. (Dessert soufflés are even more difficult: in addition to the above the cook must figure out how long people will take to finish the entrée.)

The soufflé is a doomed entity for our frazzled era. But here goes.

3 T butter
3 T flour
1 ½ cups hot milk
4 thickly beaten egg yolks
3/4 cup grated cheddar cheese
5 egg whites
Wax paper or foil

Melt butter. Add flour and stir to make a roux. Stir in the hot milk until sauce thickens. Season with pinches of salt, pepper and, if you like, nutmeg. Pour a few tablespoons of hot sauce into the yolks, stir, return all to the pot. Stir for a few seconds, turn off heat. Stir in cheese bit by bit. COOL THOROUGHLY. Beat egg whites until stiff. Fold into sauce.

Turn into a buttered 4 cup soufflé dish. Rip off a sheet of wax paper or foil to fit around the dish. Fold it in two lengthwise, tie around the dish with string so the top half extends above the top of the dish.

Bake in a preheated 375° oven 30 minutes. Remove paper collar. Serve immediately. Though the soufflé will deflate — poof! — the instant the serving spoon hits it, while it holds it is a miracle.

CRANBERRY MOLD

My friend Jini, who inhabits a tiny woodland house alongside a large tidal river, where she skinny-dips at dawn, makes this mold when she's feeling festive.

4 cups fresh cranberries
1 cup sugar
1 T unflavored gelatin
3/4 cup fresh orange juice
1 cup chopped celery
1 cup chopped peeled apple
1 cup chopped walnuts or pecans

Wash and drain cranberries, put through coarse blade of a grinder or zap briefly — do not pulverize — in a processor or blender. Stir in sugar, let stand 20 minutes. Stir again.

Stir gelatin into orange juice, heat to dissolve over low flame -- it's easier to clean up if you keep the o.j. and gelatin in a flame-proof measuring cup and put *it* inside a pot of simmering water. Add to cranberries and stir. Stir in celery, apple, nuts. Turn into 1) a very pretty glass bowl or 2) a 4-cup ring mold that's been rinsed with cold water. Refrigerate overnight.

If you have used a mold, turn confection out onto a rinsed platter. Fill center with sliced cucumbers, daisies, parsley, or other pretties.

CRISPS

In ENDLESS ENDLESS ENDLESS FEBRUARY, serve with beer in front of a hot woodstove.

1 lb cheddar cheese, grated
1/4 lb (1 stick) butter at room temperature
Pinch salt

164

2 t Worcestershire (no substitutes)
1/2 t paprika
1 cup flour

Mix everything together.

Knead and shape into a two inch wide roll, wrap in wax paper, refrigerate overnight.

Slice carefully (lopsided slices bake unevenly), place on a greased sheet, bake in a preheated 450° oven 7 minutes, or until crisp, hot and extravagantly tasty. Blot with paper towels, serve to serious acclaim.

NON EDIBLES

PLAYDOUGH

is mostly but not strictly for small children. Turn it over to preschoolers along with rolling pin, fork, spoon, cookie cutters, pie pans, old buttons, shells, paper clips and stones. Spread the work area with newspapers. Watch as such miracles as "cookies," "string," "nothing," and "turtles" emerge.

4 cups flour
1 cup salt
1 ½ cups water
Food coloring

Mix flour, salt, water. When well blended, separate dough into three or four sections. Add a few drops of coloring to each, knead 10 minutes to bring up colors.

Playdough in the hands of an older child or an adult can be shaped into Christmas tree ornaments such as angels, dancers (use a garlic press to make hair, a pizza cutter for serrated collars and hems), houses facades with see-through windows, and so on. Omit the food coloring, make certain each ornament is of uniform thickness (approximately 1/4 inch) so that no edges burn. Insert wire hooks for hanging, bake in a preheated 350° oven 1 hour. Cool before designing to your heart's content with acrylic paints. Baked playdough objects will store for two or three years.

POMANDER BALLS

Pomander balls, which function as sachets, should be made in October or November for December giving. It is a great project to do with kids and a soothing one for all. The following instructions make one pomander.

One large orange   Cinnamon
A whole lot of cloves   Orris root (available at pharmacies)

Insert cloves all over skin of orange. It is kinder to the thumb to insert each one at a slight angle. (You may also start each hole with a pick, though I have never found it necessary to do so.) The job can be spread over several sessions.

When the orange is covered with cloves, shake it in a paper bag with a heaping teaspoonful each of cinnamon and orris root powder. Wrap loosely in foil, store in a cupboard for three to four weeks or until dried and fragrant.

Tie with a thin ribbon, or layer a thinner ribbon over a slightly wider one of a different color. You can also place the pomander ball in a small net or square of calico (pinked edges) and tie with a ribbon at the neck.

FINGER PAINT

This is the messiest kind of painting children can do and my don't they love it. What's important is the communication between adult and child as the paint is created.

1/2 cup corn starch	2 cups hot water
Food coloring	1/2 cup dish detergent
1 cup cold water	5 jars with lids
1 T unflavored gelatin	Pad of large size newsprint

Dissolve corn starch in 3/4 cup cold water in a pot. Soften gelatin in remaining 1/4 cup water.

Stir hot water into corn starch mix, cook over medium heat until it boils and is clear, stirring constantly. Remove from heat, stir in gelatin mix. Stir in detergent until dissolved. Cool.

Pour five separate portions into large jars and let the child stir several generous drops of food coloring into each. Colors must be strong; the pastel shades that are rendered with just two or three drops look pretty but don't show up on paper. Suggested colors: red, blue, yellow, orange (a blend of red and yellow) and green (a blend of blue and yellow).

DRY HAIR TREATMENT

Massage warm, not hot, corn oil into hair. Wrap head in a towel. Leave one hour. Shampoo and rinse three times. Use conditioner.

Afterword On Calories

We eat while we drive the car, surf the screen, browse the mall, and walk down Main Street. But once a day we should treat ourselves to the human ritual of

> 1) companionship at table
> 2) a relationship with our food

Wholesome food is a miracle for which we owe thanks-giving, and we should bless everything that is set before us.

As for the useless word "dieting", a diet is something we go on, therefore it is something we go off. A 97% recidivism rate proves the case.

Like all living matter we take in and put out energy. We are little furnaces, and when intake exceeds output, or vice-versa, it leads to poor balance. It may be wiser to think "lack of balance" or "poor health" rather than "fat". Another overused phrase is "body image". Trash it.

Educate yourself about CALORIE OUTPUT. Working toward a positive goal of health through exercise may help you to keep more in balance than the negative goal of trying to lose something. As calorie output becomes part of your life as a no-excuses activity at a given hour, calorie intake and you may fall into better sync.

Sounds easy. It's tough. But lifelong health is a worthwhile goal to pursue, and it's the journey that counts.

Index

D

SPECIAL NOTE ON EGGS

Though some information states that only pasteurized (heated) eggs should be used in the uncooked form, in real life such eggs do not exist on the retail level. Only the food service industry uses pasteurized eggs, and the reason they can buy them and you can't is that the eggs are packaged, out of the shell, in 55-gallon drums.

BÉARNAISE SAUCE on page 53 calls for heating anyway. Be sure you cook it until one or two bubbles appear on the surface, or USE AN INSTANT READ THERMOMETER (available at housewares stores): either heat the yolks and water to 140° and keep it there for three minutes, or heat to 160° and remove from the heat right away. Stir constantly.

Classic recipes for mayonnaise and Hollandaise do not call for cooking. But according to the American Egg Board — an agency overseen by the US Department of Agriculture — the sauces will be risk-free (not cooked, only heated) if you follow the above directions.

This means that in addition to getting the blender or food processor messy, you have to get a pot messy. Better safe than sorry. Though most adults who are infected recover within days without treatment, others have been hospitalized, and a few nursing home patients have died. Persons at risk include infants, pregnant women, the elderly and anyone with an impaired immune system.

HOLLANDAISE ON PAGE 54: Before you blend the yolks, lemon juice and salt, put them in a small pot and add 2 T water. Over very low heat, stir constantly until your instant read thermometer, or your eyesight, tells you the yolks are safe (see above directions). Pour into a blender or processor and proceed as usual. MAYONNAISE ON PAGE 54: Before you process the yolks, mustard, salt and lemon juice, put them in a small pot and add 2 T water. Proceed as above. REFRIGERATE IF NOT USING IMMEDIATELY AND REFRIGERATE LEFTOVER SAUCE.

The American Egg Board has uncooked (but heated) egg recipes on its web site, www.aeb.org. You may also write to them at 1460 Renaissance Drive, Park Ridge, IL 60068, or call your state's cooperative extension office.